OUR LADY'S MESSAGE OF MERCY TO THE WORLD

The

Little Blue Diary

"I promise to take at the hour of death with My Angels that soul who, with love and devotion, reads this diary and honours My Image and Scapular and especially takes into their heart My message of June 16th 1989 'Pray for poor sinners.'"

Published by CAMPION

This paperback edition 2021

Copyright © Campion 2021

All rights reserved
A CIP catalogue record for this book
is available from the British Library

ISBN 978-1-8380386-3-2

Campion Publishers
Well House, Green Lane, Ardleigh CO7 7PD, UK

7 9 10 8 6

Printed in Poland

www.themercifulmadonna.com

OUR LADY'S MESSAGE OF MERCY TO THE WORLD

A TRUE DEVOTION TO THE IMMACULATE HEART OF MARY

Dear Queen of the World, Sovereign Lady,
to You do we give our hearts for ever. Amen

*"Loving Me doesn't detract from loving My Son,
it adds to the beauty of your soul."*

March 8 1989

CAMPION

Nihil Obstat: Dublin March 22 2000
Rev. Brendan Leahy D.D. Deputy Censor Dublin Diocese.
Printed with Ecclesiastical permission.

Our Lady's directive on the new edition.*

"The book itself is to be disseminated as quickly as possible. To allow this the following is requested that anyone wishing to print the book is requested to keep to the format and fidelity to the text. All plates inside the book may be in colour or black and white. Those that print it should take care not to go into debt. Finally do everything in a spirit of obedience and that it be distributed on the basis that it be a non-commercial issue with no specified donation."

January 9 2002

* see appendix page 623
  also page 621

Note regarding Private Revelations:
Private Revelations "do not belong to the deposit of faith. It is not their role to improve or complete Christ's definitive revelation, but to help live more fully by it in a certain period of history." (Catechism of the Catholic Church.67) However, when they lead us back to the Gospel of Jesus, private revelations can bring us into closer contact with the God of Divine Mercy, and to the wonderful graces and blessings which flow from Him and inspire us to lead lives worthy of the great love given to us freely by the God who saves.

INTRODUCTION

With reports of messages from Our Lady reaching us from all over the world, true devotees of Our Beloved Mother will pray for the grace of discernment to believe which are true and distinctive for them to follow.

When I was given the blue book of *Our Lady's Message of Mercy to the World,* reporting what Mary had requested be made known to Her children, according to the instructions, I first said a prayer. I then opened the book at random and read the 'pearl' on the left-hand page. This was the 'nub' of the particular message on the opposite page, which was intended for me at that time.

I recognised then that these consoling yet serious messages would help us to confront the difficulties and challenges of life in the New Millennium, in this increasingly God-forsaking world.

As our loving Mother, She has been assigned this unique role of giving individual messages of hope and love to Her starving children.

Since then, I have felt a new dimension to my life which I pray will enable me and others to give comfort and hope to all who thus seek the help of Our Lady Help of Christians, Queen of the Home.

May She so speak to you and bring you Her peace.

The late Stella Maris Lilley

*"My child,
make reparation your life!"*

OUR LADY VISITING THE ORATORY OF THE IMMACULATE HEART, RAHENY, DUBLIN 1989

The Image of Peace

The Merciful Madonna Mary Immaculate Mediatrix of all graces
Our Lady Queen of the Home pray for us.

Actual size of Image 203mm x 355
Our Lady requested that the Image be framed and put behind glass.

The Meaning of the Image

"Today I am going to tell you the meaning of My Image and the seven showings contained in it."

1. *The halo around My head is the twelve stars.*

2. *There is a host of Cherubs in the form of a cloud at My feet.*

3. *A Rosary of fifteen Mysteries falls from My hands joined in prayer.*

4. *My garment is clothed with the Sun.*

5. *In the folds of My left arm, Christ is crucified.*

6. *The left side of My garment is covered in the Precious Blood, which falls from the Cross of My Son, forming a brown stain*

7. *A Host is suspended over a Chalice beneath this brown stain.*

"Let him who has eyes to see, see, and let him who has faith believe. I am the Mediatrix. This is the meaning of the Image."

July 13 1995

How to use the Diary

This diary is not meant to be read from front to back. This diary is very precious. It is our tangible link with our Blessed Mother in Heaven. The way to use this diary is as Our Lady has said, *"Pray before reading My messages."* Say a prayer, any prayer of your choice, then open the diary at random and read the message through for that date. This message is Our Lady's personal message to you.

Our Lady has said of this diary: -

"Have no fear. You must concentrate only on the book I have given you. Delete nothing Providence has revealed to you. St. Joseph will guard it in purity and I will guard it in maternity. It will be a star that will shine out for all the world to see and a fresh breeze blowing through the Church. Never before in the history of the Church have I blessed such a book as I have the one I have given you. Truly My Image is the Mediatrix of all graces. Pray! Pray! In prayer you will obtain everything."

Oct. 24 1997

"In essence, the book of messages is for the renewal of every soul ."

Apr. 2 1998.

"If you pray, you will find the answer to every situation that has no peace and where no peace can be found. Open the messages and ask Me what message I want you to live each day and I will tell you. I ask you not to live the messages of the world but live My messages and you will find peace, and they will spread and you will be truly happy, and everyone will see in you the reflection of My messages."

Jan.14 1999

"I have given you the greatest sign that I am truly with you in every situation. This sign is, that I speak to you when you open the book. In this way I help you believe with your heart."

Jan. 31 1999

"Abandon yourself to My Immaculate Heart. In that way you will be able to overcome every evil that threatens you. You do this by opening the book and reading My messages every day. Let them change you. In this way you will experience the graces God wishes to give you through them. It is for this reason I am speaking to you through them, but you must listen with your heart if you are to comprehend My words."

Feb. 1 1999

"Again I remind you to simply open the book at any page and you will find the path that leads to peace and know an indescribable joy."

Mar. 11 1999

"When you hold the book, you hold Me, your Mediatrix of all Grace. At any moment no matter where you are and you feel worried or you have lost your peace or you simply need Me, open the book at any page and follow My words and in that moment you will experience that deep calm that is within My Immaculate Heart."

Apr. 19 1999

This diary is also a great comfort when you are particularly worried or upset about events in your life, as Our Lady has said, *"When you need Me, open the book."* Let Our Lady guide you, especially now in this special time of the 2000th Anniversary of Her dear Son Our Lord Jesus Christ's birth. May the good and Merciful Lord and His Heavenly Mother bless you.

A.M. † D.G.

What, may you ask, is this diary all about? It is to be simple and how to live simply with God who longs to live in our hearts just as much as in the time when Saints like St. Francis walked the roads of his native Italy.

Our Lady is no stranger to this world of today. She offers mankind again the message of Her Son, that it should live in our hearts, and that we spread it to all without pomp, but as Our Lady would have us spread it, in all the little things of our lives.

This message is eternal life and Our Lady is offering us this gift through Her Message of Mercy that She may lift our burdens and help us *"Begin anew"* and look to Her as our guide through the darkness of this world to the light of Heaven.

OUR LADY'S MESSAGE OF MERCY TO THE WORLD

"My dear little one, I smile on you even though you think you are wounded beyond repair. No one is beyond repair, only those that wish to stay that way!"

Feb.14 1992

"Know that I am the Mother who leads you to My Son Jesus."

1989

Jan. 14–"Dear child, before I led you on a path of purification. Now I lead you in secret on a path of interior captivity.

You don't know what I mean, but if you accept these locutions, you will come **to** *know that I am the Mother who leads you to My Son Jesus.*"

"Come to the foot of the Cross."

Jan.15–"Dear child, when I come I cause My children to be aware of My faith, that they may be heightened in their faith.

If you *come to the foot of the Cross*, you will know joy and peace will flood your soul, because it is at the foot of the Cross one really meets My Son Jesus."

"Often you forget I am even there."

Jan. 16–"My dear child, look and think of how I lavish on you so much attention.

Often you forget I am even there. I am moving among all the little things of your life, they are My delight. Refuse Me no corner where I can clean and help keep tidy for you.

You need so much to know I am ordering all the details of your life. Not a moment goes by that I don't know about with you."

*"Let Me teach you the ways
of infinite beauty."*

Jan. 17–"Dear child, look at My Son bleeding on the Cross. He dies so that men might live a life free from the tyranny of sin.

Don't let this moment pass without thinking of this. My love is so great for you. *Let Me teach you the ways of infinite beauty*.*"

* God's grace

"It is now My designs and the pattern you must be attentive to."

Jan. 18–"My dear child, you grasp and try by your own intellect to carry out what God is asking of you, but you fail and think *'is there any way?'*

Are you not aware *it is now My designs and the pattern you must be attentive to*? All else is vanity and will vanish like the morning mist before the heat of the sun.

Pray and pray and simply pray as to no end. Simply put your trust in Me, your Mother and all the trials you will face, you will face with prayer."

"Come closer to Me."

Jan. 19–"Dear child, it is only when you *come closer to Me* that you can visualise Jesus.

You are aware that I, the Mother, am the only one to help you live in Jesus perfectly.

So pray to Me, the Mother of your soul, that you may understand all that I am doing in your life."

*"One and one only should
occupy your soul
Jesus."*

Jan. 20–"Dear child, *one and one only should occupy your soul, Jesus.*

How do you find Him? Through Me who is Mother of your soul.

Influenced by all else is not good. It takes your heart from Me. Nothing can give you peace. Only My way, through Me."

"Don't rush around looking for the next event to hit you."

Jan. 21–"Dear child, *don't rush around looking for the next event to hit you*. The event already has! It already has! Live it! It is each moment God allows to you. Pray.

Let understanding be for those whose business it is to understand. Do not react but let go. God already knows your heart and so do I, so do I My child."

"Listen and pray. I am calling you again."

Jan. 22–"Dear child, so *listen and pray. I am calling you again* to renew your life.

Begin again to let Me plan it from moment to moment, to let Me guide you safely through to your true home in Heaven.

Don't get involved in anything other than God's work. Now, respond by letting Me be Mother of your soul!"

"Do not hide from Me your wretchedness."

Jan. 23–"Oh My dear child, did you not understand the simplicity of all that I do for you? By My Motherhood of you, you are mine.

Even though you fail at times, this is to be expected, but *do not hide from Me your wretchedness* when you do.

Bring your shame to Me so that I can console you and help you in your faith which has been weakened. Surrender yourself to Me, thus you will be made strong by My love."

"You have little time for frivolities."

Jan. 24–"Dear little child, evening is upon you and the storm is about to blow and *you have little time for frivolities.*

Only My presence can save you from the ambushes the Devil lays for you. This is because you have responded to My call.

How beautiful is God that He grants you such favour in these locutions so as you hear My voice and wish only to be led by Me, your Queen and Holy Mother. This is indeed a wonder."

"Come to Me in your heart whenever you need Me."

Jan. 25–"Dear child, *come to Me in your heart whenever you need Me.* I will be there to rescue you and comfort you.

You should be glad that I have chosen you to be a special instrument to show the world My sweetness towards My little souls.

Through you someday, I wish to gather a valiant amount of little souls who will consecrate themselves to Me for the sake of those souls* who feel left out in the cold, that they are loved just as much with My Maternal love."

---

* Poor sinners

*"Offer to Me all your misgivings
and longings."*

Jan. 26–"My child, follow Me in My faith. *Offer to Me all your misgivings and longings.*

Do all for Me. I will mother you back to full strength, to full joy! Thus My joy may be complete to see you at last truly My child who has My grace.

To be so much all the more poorer in everything for My sake is a treasure that I can offer to God. Offer to Me this treasure, the treasure of your poverty, for Me to do with what I will."

"Today I have something for you to be aware of."

Jan. 27–"My child, *today I have something for you to be aware of.* The indifference paid to Me causes God much pain, but with one Our Father – Hail Mary – and Glory be to the Father – prayed to this end (with all your heart) to help redress this pain and help convert those who cause this sadness;

If you do this everyday before My Son in the Blessed Sacrament, you will win great graces for those whose hearts have little or no faith — all through Me!"

"With prayer open your heart wide."

Jan. 28–"My sweet little one, pray one *Ave* for My children so far away from Me, who long for such faith that is granted to you today.

Pray, and *with prayer open your heart wide* to all who silently wait alone, the poor ones who are weary. Pray and remember those who wish to know the faith.

I invite you! See My love. How you have been made strong and sensitive to your own belief."

"My grace is sufficient for you."

Jan. 29–"My sweet little one, *My grace is sufficient for you.* Show Me your willingness to be with Me.

I will show you My Son, who has given Me the office of leading you, with Me, to Him.

By this new way I wish you to confide in Me before you do anything and I shall tell you what to do."

"I dearly wish to lead you."

Jan. 30–"My child, My little one so torn between the world and My offer of total austerity. If only you knew how *I dearly wish to lead you* along this path travelled by so few. Lay at My feet your Amen. Depend totally on Me. Listen to Me.

Allow no other way take your fancy, or luring of any worldly kind. But seek with Me My fine jewel* of great price and do not stop until you are satisfied. My little one, to know truly My union with you, you must shed first vain thoughts and seek that which seems not so kind to your nature, but which is at war with your soul.

Let this seed grow in your soul, taking care of it like you would a young sapling, making sure nothing damages it. This is but the beginnings."

---

* A clean heart

"Dear little one, don't be discouraged."

Jan. 31–"My child, My *dear little one, don't be discouraged* when you fall.

Rely on My mercy, with My Son, to grant you the grace to calmly admit your sin and bravely continue with courage."

"Continue to pray. Let nothing trouble you."

Feb. 1–"My little one, so many have wished to be this close and yet to you this grace has been granted.

Because of this, I have gained for you such grace and am gaining much more to help you carry out My little plan in your soul, so that My wonders are spoken of from generation to generation.

Continue to pray. Let nothing trouble you, even your weakness."

"Pray and long for Eternal things."

Feb. 2–"Dear little one, when have I so much wanted more a soul to respond than I have yours. And how can you think I would abandon you? If you have any sorrow, let Me be the one to heal it.

It would be much longer to reach My Son by any other way than the way that I am leading you.

Pray and long for Eternal things. Leave everything else aside."

"Be but patient."

Feb. 3–"Dear little one, how to be loving to My Son is the longing of many.

But how sad it is to see how much they go astray when some calamity befalls them.

If they would but realise that they are loved much more if they would *be but patient.*"

"No matter how hard you find it, battle on and pray."

Feb. 4–"Dear little one, the way of the world is so far along the road to perdition. There is little hope, but God's Justice.

Mankind has fallen to its lowest depths and it shall be only by a supernatural intervention that can save him. Otherwise he will lay waste his soul to the slavery of Satan.

That is why your slavery to Me is so precious. *No matter how hard you find it, battle on and pray.*"

"Don't worry, My little one."

Feb. 5–"Dear little one, I haven't forgotten how little you are. This is such a beautiful time we have together. Let us not think of our weakness but rather God's mercy.

Don't worry, My little one, I can see further along the road. You have so much to learn. I am making of you a little angel.

You see, I love you beyond your sin and its density in your soul. So little one, don't be afraid to come to Me."

*"From My Heart, I invite men
to turn from sin."*

Feb. 6–"My little one, *from My Heart, I invite men to turn from sin* and follow the way of the Holy Gospel, letting Me be their guiding Mother through the darkness of this world to the light of Heaven.

Come with Me. Decide today to follow Me as I speak to your heart.

Come everyday to meet Me and My Son Jesus He wants you to listen to My message."

"Believe it is I."

Feb. 7–"My child, when you worry, I cry. When you sin, you hurt Me. When you try to be good, I pray for you so that you will be better.

I am your Mother. As a Mother I think only of how I can save you from taking the road that is wide and many souls take. You see I know men's hearts and I know how they fool themselves. The road I lead you on is full of thorns but is full of sweetness you have never felt. Sin no more! Tomorrow shall be your Baptism of Fire.

Renew your life. *Believe it is I.* Just you and Me. No one can guide you to the beauty of Heaven with more certainty than Me."

"I have a great grace for you."

Feb. 8–"My child, today *I have a great grace for you,* but pray that you open to its power to change you. Knowing you personally as I do, I want you to experience to the fullest the efficacy of this grace, which I give you.

Remain in the interior of your soul today this is where you will find Me always. This is prayer from the heart.

Return often during the day to this altar in your soul. There you will know My Love."

"Seek the way of holiness and desire to grow hidden."

Feb.9–"My child, today I invite you consider the way of men who are blinded by riches, power and self-seeking pleasure. This is what leads to the destruction of their souls.

Be as free as a bird, drawn not to the wants of men but given up to the pursuit of spiritual and eternal things.

Seek the way of holiness and desire to grow hidden in the example of My Son who had poverty and oppression as His friends."

"In all, allow peace."

Feb.10–"My child, resist the malediction that to battle in all conflicts and arguments with men is your calling as My child.

No! to win any battle, prayer must be from the start and patience must be its end. *In all, allow peace.*

Being aware of any other outcome in the battle against evil is only made by My hand, to win souls and to do so in My way. To think any other way is wrong."

"I am the one who leads to holiness."

Feb. 11–"My child, to know Me is genuine holiness. *I am the one who leads to holiness.*

My little one, pray that this rare gift be your one desire that you be like Me.

If you shall come to Me, you will receive what you most dearly want. For nowhere else will you find true happiness."

*"Renew your resolutions
and begin again."*

Feb. 12–"My child, even though the temptations are too strong and you fail, strength will be given to you to *renew your resolutions and begin again.* It is in the battle a soldier must not desert, so too you must continue for My love.

This is the greatest of all gallantry that one should lay down his life for those whom he loves. Prove your love. Be prepared no matter the wounds.

Look to the true life, the life that has My love as its goal, and do not accept any other. My little one, you will fight and be brave to the end."

"Leave everything in My hands and My mercy."

Feb. 13–"My child, if sin prevails in your life it is because you lack turbulence within your soul, in order to shake loose from its bond. The time will come when you will no longer need to rationalise* what is happening within your soul.

I will help you produce fruit that will cause sin to die in your life, but first you must not constantly look at the sin, but My little one, unleash your soul from its bond and walk towards Me slowly.

But do not look back or try to remember anything about your sin. *Leave everything in My hands and My mercy.*"

* doubt

"Never tire of asking My help."

Feb. 14—"My child, between Me and you are strewn flowers of a great variety. Many you fail to pick up. Many you fail to see due to lack of desire.

If you really wish to perceive of My delights, you have to give in to Me, even to the very needs of your body and soul. Handing them over is not enough, but willing only to breathe Me in them is what really matters. Pray. Pray. *Never tire of asking My help.*"

*"Reserve to Me the right to do
with you whatever."*

Feb.15–"My child, do *reserve to Me the right to do with you whatever* I will. It is in this that benefits the Mystical Body of My Son. To grow more and more like Me is including the Body of My Son.

It is of vital importance you continue, no matter the consequence, in prayer. To refrain or fade in this would be fatal. Only through prayer can I reach you and you Me."

*"No one has come to Me and
left empty-handed."*

Feb. 16–"My child, *no one has come to Me and left empty-handed.*

But for you whom I grant to write down My messages, I avail so much to draw you on, even though you feel discouraged. Let not this feeling cause you to become impatient.

It is for this very reason I left you to finish your Rosary today. To be patient is waiting on Me as one who has no other means of support."

"Men wish to avoid tribulations."

Feb. 17–"My child, wander not onto paths that appear good but happen to be wrong.* They are full of pride, power and ways of the world. Stay close to Me. Be careful not to approach other highways.

You will know My highway because it has many thorns and is full of that which *men wish to avoid–tribulations!* which cause the soul to rise and long for Heaven, heeding not the wisdom of this world."

* Proverbs 14:12

"Continue to listen."

Feb. 18–"My child, true wisdom comes from Me and if you will *continue to listen,* I shall lead you into the most magnificent garden where your soul may drink great draughts for the nourishment of your soul and there you will find true joy."

"You may not understand all."

Feb. 19–"My child, pleasing or not to Me, you are still My little one. I love you. No one shall separate you from My love.

Be unsuited, as you may think, for any purpose I may have in mind, will not change even in the slightest, the wonders I shall work in your poor little soul.

My little one *you may not understand all* the secrets I will work in your soul. But do not try. It is enough you know."

"Place your soul at My disposal."

Feb. 19–"My child, try not be too hasty in running after spiritual heights.

Wake to move less to be pleased in consolation than be pleasing to Me in poverty of spirit. True devotion is inner and void of feeling.

Do not think I am in any way unhappy with you if you fail to feel any experience. This is what leads to what is shallow and full of emptiness.

Place your soul at My disposal, for now the rehearsal is over. Now begins the play on the stage of life for your soul."

"Build in your soul a great devotion to Me."

Feb. 20–"My child, sow in the garden of your soul the precious seed of My grace.

Help Me to help you come to the altar of repose within you and there place the offering of your past with all its sorrows and joys.

My little one, *build in your soul a great devotion to Me* and come daily to replenish from its fountain of My love."

"Pray and believe that you are heard."

Feb. 21–"My child, no time spent in front of My Son is ever wasted, although you may not know its outcome. It's not for you to know these things. It's for you to *pray and believe that you are heard*.

My little one, don't become discouraged at the least thing. Life is too short. Trust in Me like a child at its mother's knee. It is here My Son will grant you His blessing. Refuse Him nothing."

"God smiles on you."

Feb. 22–"My child, *God smiles on you* when you refrain from wanting all that is so important in this world and look to that which seems too foolish for man.

When you lay at My feet all broken I take great care that you go away whole. It is My office to make men whole again."

*"Do not let Satan snatch the gifts
God gives you."*

Feb. 23–"My child, be full of great expectations at this time when God is giving special graces to those who call upon Me. I can only help you if you respond to Me, otherwise you close the door on God's gifts if you think little of My love.

God is calling you to a great renewal of your life. Decide for Him today and make Me happy. *Do not let Satan snatch the gifts God gives you* at this time. Pray that you hold on to My Mantle.

I am inviting you, My little one, to a deeper level of prayer in your life. Respond and receive My gift with love."

*"Only in prayer can you learn
how to be good."*

Feb. 25–"My child, *only in prayer can you learn how to be good*.

The Holy Mass must be lived and the centre of your life. There you have Heaven.

My little one, I invite you to be prayerful during My Son's Passion. God will give, if you ask with love, special graces during this time.* Pray with love."

---

* During Mass

"Your only comfort is in prayer."

Feb. 26–"My child, the love you bear Me is sweetness to My Heart and it makes My Son very happy, because He now has a tent where He can rest from the battle.

You have been blessed by Me and My love. Represent Me to all by your recollection of Me in your soul. When you have done this you will know peace.

Pray with hope. My little one so weak, now you have been left to taste the flower of pain and isolation, and now you find *your only comfort is in prayer*. My child, the beads are so precious. Let them be your only introduction to the Heavenly staircase.

My little one, remain little. The more you seek creatures, the more your pain will be. Pray, pray and keep watch with My Son who watches you closely."

"Heaven, the last Altar where your soul will find true joy."

Feb. 27–"My child, My love has you spellbound, this is as it should be. Listen, My little one. If you do wish to be totally My child, then allow Me to send you the lilies of My Son's agony.

I invite you. Accept graciously suffering from My hand. It will lead you to *Heaven, the last Altar where your soul will find true joy.* To advance in holiness, you must accept with joy, the trials God sends you."

"I am still with you."

Feb. 28–"My child, brilliant though the rays of the sun are, they cannot compare with the graces I grant you.

Pray that you take no respite in the battle, even if you feel all have left you.

I am still with you."

"Don't be annoyed when you are usurped in little ways."

Mar. 1–"My child, I invite you to break this unbridled want to be adept at worldly pursuits.

Pray to be let loose from this bond which can only aggravate your soul, thus you lose your peace.

My little one, *don't be annoyed when you are usurped in little ways*. These are stepping stones to grace. Receive them with love."

*"To be holy is the true essence
of Mother Church. "*

Mar. 3–"My child, if you wish to be a Saint then come and look at the Cross. There, is the great teaching! To hold faith and want *to be holy is the true essence of Mother Church.*

My little one, being led merely to receive a reward trivialises all that My Son went through for you. Wanting to love as much as you can, Me and My Son, is true appreciation of the pain He went through for you.

Don't let moments pass when you can show Me how much you love Me. Send Me little blossoms of your helplessness. These I will treasure and give a value beyond their worth"

"My sweetness is pure and comes from Heaven."

Mar. 4–"My child, weakness is strength in the way of My Son. It makes man docile and conscious of his destiny.

Where would you find such peace as you do in My arms, My little one? Only by My love will you see the wonder of all that I do for you. *My sweetness is pure and comes from Heaven.*

I invite you. Do not doubt the words. You sadden Me when, like a lake that longs for salt water, you long for such that is transitory. My child, you should pour out grave doubts at My feet. I shall deal with them in My own way."

"Being little entails being trampled on!"

Mar.4–"My child, *being little entails being trampled on!*"

"Pray well."

Mar. 5–"My child, begin each dialogue with Me by asking Me how to *pray well.* Then I shall hold you constantly all the way through. That way you will be truly praying and you will enjoy it.

My little one, if you are in any way short with souls, it is because you run with the tide. Turn to Me the next time you feel like this.

My child, I will do from now on your thinking and I will set out all the small and big events of your life. My little one, say hello for Me to (---)."

"Be patient and trust in Me."

Mar. 5–"I know at times it seems all too high and far away and you think *'Will I ever get there?'*

My little one, *be patient and trust in Me.* You will !"

"Pray, trust and know I am near."

Mar. 7–"My little one, one thing should break through your cloud of trials and you should hold on to it. That is, if I invite you to let you hear My voice inside you, this! – whatever is happening around you–is what should take greater importance nothing else should trouble you.

Only My words are the important thing, on these you should rest. Nowhere can you find greater comfort than in these words. They are your joy. My little one, *pray, trust, and know I am near.*

When My child you think you have no strength left, I will anoint you with the oil of My love. Is it not a true Mother that loves and loves and loves? I, My child, love you more than this."

"Let it come from your heart."

Mar. 8–'*I was thinking how mechanical my prayer was.*'
"*Let it come from your heart* then it becomes an offering of infinite value."

"You should exercise faith."

Mar. 8–'*I was doubting*'.
"The more you doubt My words, the more *you should exercise faith*."

"Sinners have drifted away from My love."

Mar. 8–"My child thank you for coming. You don't know how I long to hear your footsteps to the door of My Heart. I want you to be My confidante, the comforter of My Heart. How I long to have these chats with you. You help ease My pain.

So many *sinners have drifted away from My love* and now see no way back to My Heart. But you! My little instrument, offer Me your nothingness. This is so precious to Me, even more precious than if you were to pray non-stop.

If only souls knew how their very weakness is their very strength, because it draws down on them My Son's loving glance. Pray that you stay close to My Heart in your littleness."

"Become small."

Mar. 10–"My child, the reason I wait for you to pray your beads is so that you don't feel you've prayed improperly. I talk to you. Let Me continue to talk to you whenever I give you the rendezvous, as I do, after you have prayed your beads.

I am leading you. Open the door more often to Me, the door of contemplation. My little one, time is moving on. Eternity gets closer. I value more and more our little chats. *Become small.* Each little thing, do it in Me."

"I am humility."

Mar. 11–"Hello My child. Blind though you are, let Me lead you trustingly.

This is how Jesus would have you, rather than slithering along open-eyed, enchanted by every desire that came to your inner soul. You understand? My little one, yearn for Love's desire to consume your inner soul. Allow no reptiles to enter. Drive them off the moment you see them approach. Pray *'O Virgin, defend me.'* Answer them thus.

Cold though your soul is, I sincerely wish to stay there. *I am Humility*. Tread softly when you enter the inner soul. Jesus is asleep there. Pray hymns and you cover Him with blankets and keep Him warm. This is love, Love's wisdom.

Reflect Me by loving everyone, most of all they that hurt you."

"Pray, even if you are annihilated."

Mar. 12–"Hello My little one. *Pray, even if you are annihilated* by temptations. Pray, even if sweetness abandons you and you feel nothing but dryness. Pray.

It is only in the act of praying I bless you, and it is while praying, grace is bestowed on you, so pray. Pray. Pray!"

"Only God raises the soul."

Mar. 12–"Hello My child. It is only by grace that a soul can attain perfection, Love's great desire.

Only God raises the soul. No soul however that soul tries, will ever reach holiness without grace.

If but that soul would place in My hands its longing, I let the soul, however weak, touch God's very throne and help it reach Heaven."

"You must allow Me to destroy sin in your life."

Mar. 13–"My child, God has bestowed so many favours on you and He wishes to bestow many more, but *you must allow Me to destroy sin in your life* thus I may lead you to the everlasting joy of Heaven."

"Remain close to Me."

Mar. 13–"My little one, rest in My love. There is your altar of repose. I wish your soul to rise above this earth and taste the sweetness of Heaven. My child, My dear one, *remain close to Me*, close to the Heart of your Mother who consoles you in all your trials.

Today, My child, I invite you to take up the flame of love and seal it upon your heart. You will know what it is. I give it to you now. It is the love you bear Me. This love I will cause to grow in your cold heart, until it becomes a fire of great strength that will burn unto eternity in your breast.

My poor instrument, pray to Me so that I can mould you and keep you safe from the clutches of My adversary, who thinks only on how to destroy you."

"Open the door of your heart."

Mar. 14–'*Mary help me.*'
"My dearest little one, *open the door of your heart to Me* and don't be afraid to love Me with all of your soul. This is what gives God the greatest glory, to love Him through My Heart.

Oh My child, so fainthearted, do you not understand that your love for Me is augmented and embellished and given to Jesus for His greater glory.

My dear child, place at My disposal everything, even your littlest actions, so that Jesus can look and be charmed by their beauty. The littlest action, My child, what joy you give to Him when you do it for Me. You understand?"

"Look to Me for all your needs."

Mar. 16–"Hello My child. Thank you for coming. When you come, I am happy to see you so that I can bless you. You are mine and I have a special love for you close to My Heart, united to that of My Son, who is loving you so much these days. These are the times God's grace is poured on you, when you spend them with Me and My Son.

Look to Me for all your needs. Then you will not be disappointed. My child, I bless you.

Be strong in the love you bear Me. It is so precious for Me to see you come everyday. I love you, My child, and I am leading you to My Son, the joy of your life."

"Purify your intention."

Mar. 17–"Thank you for coming, My child. Rest in My Immaculate Heart. This is where you belong, My little one, from now on, in Me.

Eternity beckons you. Is it only My love and My love alone that draws you?

Purify your intention, then you become like incense before My Son."

"Imitate Me."

Mar. 18–"Keep nothing for yourself. *Imitate Me.*"

"Think of Heaven."

Mar. 19–"My child, raise your thoughts above this earth. *Think of Heaven.* All else is gross insecurity and leaves you empty."

"I am always in your heart."

Mar. 20–'*Where are you now?*'
"*I am always in your heart* or rather you are always in mine. Draw comfort from this thought."

"I protect your soul."

Mar. 21–"Hello My child. Thank you for waiting expectantly. My Heart warms to you when you wait patiently for My love. You see how I long to speak to you, how I allow you to hear My voice. Am I not sweetness itself? Don't I glow in your heart when we are in union – Heart to heart, your hand in Mine, Me holding you, helping you brave the roughness of life and its hardships?

Do you not think I am capable of leading you through life's little trials? God has placed Me sure and a buttress against any storm. Is there any safer place than My Heart? *I protect your soul* if you place it in My hands. Give it to Me now, this moment!"

"I am here waiting."

Mar. 22–"See how My child, how easy it is to call on Me. Don't be afraid. *I am here waiting* on you even with My arms open ready. You don't even have to call. Just look at Me.

You don't imagine Me. I am in your own heart. This is My Heart. You beat within My Heart. Every thought I see. Every little glance I know. There is even no dream you have dreamt that I do not know about. So please, just call! Long for Me and I'll be there waiting. Need I explain more? Simple isn't it?"

"I am every tiny corner of your day."

Mar. 23–"You, My child, pray the *'Salve Regina'* yet you fail to see My prayer at work in your life.

It is on every fence, on every road, on those you talk to. Don't you see that, in your heart, in your soul, is My mercy, My sweetness and the hope I give you.

You come, I answer. You weep, I console. It should be your very centre of life, My all-embracing love for you. Can't you see it? It's everywhere. *I am every tiny corner of your day* in this valley of tears. Place in My hands, not your mind but your heart."

"You are ready too easily to reject My messages the moment the body is threatened in some worldly way."

Mar. 25–"My child, in all My little chats with you, I have stressed the importance of our union. My love is for you. Sometimes you don't even think of how much I love you.

You are ready too easily to reject My messages the moment the body is threatened in some worldly way.

My child, My love encompasses all of your life, even till later on, when you will see Me face to face. So please, don't worry about anything – just you and Me."

"Allow Me be your resting place."

Mar. 26–"My little one, if you would only *allow Me be your resting place,* I could transform each moment for you."

*"I come with Heaven's scent
to lift the veil."*

Mar. 26–"It is only by My love will you grow to want what is eternal. After all, *I come with Heaven's scent to lift the veil,* as it were, on the invisible and beauty of My appellation with you. Do you see?

Each little corner you give to Me of your life, I transform into glory for you.

Trust Me. Give. Learn to want Me. Tell Me you want My love. I love you more than you could ever love Me. Did I not come to you first? Well! Take My hand! Let Me lead where I will with you."

"I am loving you now."

Mar. 28–"Hello! I listen, I pray. I listen, I intercede. *I am loving you now* – Is there anymore you need?"

*"You may be ridiculed ...
this should not matter."*

Mar. 29–"Write! You may be misunderstood. *You may be ridiculed this should not matter.* Only My sweetness will sustain you. Do not become disconcerted at anything. It is from My hand and is meant to help you build up in virtue.

Pray to Me that you may come more often to Me and Jesus. I offer you this time to be as close as you wish to the Queen of your soul. I am inviting your soul to move away from the world and rise to Heaven, but only if you respond.

Your soul must be tested before it can taste the dart of My Son. It is not to every soul this beauty is made known. Make yourself My willing slave, then you may enter this place of places. Thank you, My little one. Learn more this abandonment. Oh! My little one. Do not try and smother this little voice, this is Satan deceiving you. Pray. Love My voice and it will grow like a seed in your heart until it affects all you do and say and wish. Let it grow. Write! Write! Pray!"

"I know how disbelieving you think it all is."

Mar. 29–"Hello! Hello! Don't be afraid! You know I am with you keeping you safe. Let it assume greater importance, Me with you! It's what makes you live with greater awareness of Heaven all around you. This is only because I stay with you.

Do you know how many steps you take to reach Me? I make it easy for you. *I know how disbelieving you think it all is.* Look at your room, it resembles your heart, yet I come. Don't look around you when you hear My voice. It's in your very soul.

Ask of Me how to climb the way of sanctity. You are called. It is for you! Keep Me in your young little soul."

*"Return to the depths of your soul,
return often."*

Mar. 30–"You perceived Me at work in you today. Did you?" *'Yes'*

"Closely guard all I tell you. It is full of Heavenly secrets and flowing with the dew of My Son's unction. You will find that only in Me and writing down with a joy, My words, in your soul. What a breath-taking beauty resides in you, Me! If only I could lift the veil a little more but you would die with delight if I did.

Flee the world and long to *return to the depths of your soul, return often.* This is where you belong. You won't find what you are looking for in the world.

Only inside you will you come to see real joy! If you don't write, then how will you come to know that writing My words are your delight."

"It is to the weak and little ones of this world God reveals Himself."

Mar. 30–"My little one, pray, listen and be open. Can a stone be open if it is left to gather moss?* So too, you must be ready to be industrious when it comes to your soul. I teach you Heavenly things, but you must resolutely make room in your heart for Me.

My child, being little is your charm. I know you have little worth, but it is of no importance because *it is to the weak and little ones of this world God reveals Himself*. Pray and continue on."

---

* The moss of this world.

*"You do not deceive yourself
in hearing My voice."*

Mar. 31–'*Oh Mary, I am here with you, help me.*'
"Hello My young little soul. Can I not leave you for one moment that you need Me so? But you have so much little understood My being your little voice. Pray that you have My warmth. I could not leave you. Would you leave a sick bird at the side of the road?

No one has as much compassion as I. *You do not deceive yourself in hearing My voice.* Let it draw you deeper into this Heavenly place, deep in your soul. It yearns to be heard, My voice so few want to listen to God calling them. There are now so many distracting dialogues. Men have lost their souls to the twists and turns of this world's Mammon. He no longer finds joy in himself, his very soul. He no longer recognises the voice of God inside him. But you have found this secret place, this altar of repose.

Place all your doubts and worries on this altar. I have been with you now for reasons of which you know very little. This is as it should be. To you it is given the urge to write, but why is for later on. I have let you in. This is enough for you. Trust Me and be willing to write on. It's Me. It's really Me."

*"My love is a free blown sail. Hoist your
jib and catch My love gusting
like the wind in your soul."*

Mar. 31—"This is My Heart wanting you to come closer to Me. Do you not feel that I call you sometimes. I love coming to visit your soul, so small! I never hesitate to loosen the formal approach you think I should have with you, because I am the Queen of Heaven.

I wish to be as informal with you as any mother is with her child. Remember when I came before, unannounced as it were you were trying to fight Me! How you did not think that I could be so condescending! *My love is a free blown sail. Hoist your jib and catch My love gusting like the wind in your soul.*

This is how you should be always, expecting Me to invite Myself into your daily routine. Expect Me!"

"God longs to grow in all My children's hearts."

Apr. 1–"Hello! I am here with you. Could I not ask of you one little sacrifice today? Isn't this your reward? You know that if I don't come you can help Me by offering it. Love Me with these little orchids. They are your gifts to Me. I give them to My Son.

My little one, the vast belt of rain that moves across the city should be a reminder of how much *God longs to grow in all My children's hearts.* Under this cloud there is hidden a longing for God. Pray for it so that you too may be caught out in this outburst as you were this evening. Convert to My maternal touch. Desire! Look for Me always as I look for you in your soul."

"Be always at peace."

Apr. 2–"Hello My child. Thank you for coming. *Be always at peace*. I become your little sent letter to everyone who will read Me.

Repent of every doubt. Place your little impatiences into My hand. My sweet young child, cradle My love in your heart. It will keep you warm."

"Let Me take all your little distractions."

Apr. 6–"Hello My little one. Remember that only prayer is that which keeps you open to Me. By My little voice I sweeten your day. Where would you be if you had not My affection? Could anyone give you more, or give you your heart's delight? My sweet child, I tuck you in as it were each night and bless you in the morning with My presence.

Is it not for you I wait each moment, for a little look from My little one. I long to hear you call so as I can invite Myself in. My little one, smile with My smile at everyone tomorrow and see their hearts light up.

I listen all the more to you if you are sad or full of worries. Don't think I grow weary of you, I never. My sweet child, *let Me take all your little distractions*, then I can put Me instead in their place. So simple!"

*"Offer even your inadequacies
these I turn to gold for you."*

Apr. 9–"Thank you for coming, My child. Your littleness should be enhanced by your own prayer. You let too many lizards past the door, thus you're not as dependent on Me as I would have liked.

Pray against all these intrusions. My little one, grace is given when you try to hold on to Me.

Don't think you have not much to offer Me. When you are thinking this way, *offer even your inadequacies, these I turn to gold for you,* just as I did your Rosary beads even though you had only started to pray, but I am gracious like that to you. I am a real Mother to you, am I not?"

*"I let not even your smallest worry
go astray."*

Apr. 10–"Write, My child! You were brought this evening. I called you. Did you hear Me?"
'Yes Mary, was that you?'

"My little one, so full of little earthly confusions about things, people and happenings, and things that might occur. I settle everything. You must learn to leave all these things in My care.

If you would only cease to let them carry you off and remember I am greater. Me! *I let not even your smallest worry go astray* that I do not tend to. Put your whole self under My protection."

"Drift through each day as though you had no rudder but Me."

Apr. 11–"My little one, *drift through each day as though you had no rudder but Me.*"

"You are nothing without Me."

Apr. 11–"Hello! I am very much a Mother to you. You see how I mingle in with so many of your ups and downs. How your day takes on a new dimension as it were in Me. My little one, you are so small. Even if I left you for a moment you would go bankrupt in everything, no longer would you want to reach Heaven, even little victories!

My little one, you need Me. Don't wait till you have exhausted yourself and all other avenues before you realise *you are nothing without Me.* You can't achieve it alone. No harvest will you reap without Me.

When will you come to fully depend on Me? What proofs must I show you? How weak you are. Don't be surprised at this.

When will you be ready to say *'I am Yours. Come!'* My grace is here. Alone you cannot do it."

"Don't be worried when you are trampled on."

Apr. 13–"My dear little child. Pray! God gives you special graces when you pray My Rosary.

My poor little one, *don't be worried when you are trampled on* by Satan. Help is never far away, but you must be patient and wait on Me. My little one, I bless you. Pray!"

*"I trace with My love a golden chain
over your humdrum existence."*

Apr. 13–"Hello My little child. These moments we have, they are like rare discoveries, are they not? *I trace with My love a golden chain over your humdrum existence*, a brilliance so unearthly that even the Angels are filled with delight.

Yet you doubt! It seems so, that you don't know how it can be so hidden. But I assure you, even if the sun failed to rise tomorrow, it would be a pale comparison to what Me and you are doing right now."

"Don't try to be always on top of things."

Apr. 13–"My little one, you are very small. *Don't try to be always on top of things.*

Many times you will feel lost. Trust Me. To Me you are never lost.

A drop in the tide of human existence you may be, but to Me a very precious drop!"

"Isn't love the greatest!"

Apr. 14–"My little one, do you always have to find a reason for your existence? *Isn't love the greatest!*"

"Decide to want to look at Me."

Apr. 14–"Hello My little one. Take My grace, I offer it to you every day. Ask! and I'll illuminate your poor soul with My wisdom, foolish in men's eyes but clearer than the noon-day sun. It sheds light into the dark corners of your soul.

Pray, and every kind of woe will be lifted from you. My child, nowhere will lilies grow if you do not cultivate your longing to be near Me. God's mercy is given when you look to Me. I allow (---) to perceive of My Heavenly dew with you. This should be a joy to you. Pray! I cannot emphasise the need more. You are so much taken these days by the least breath from Me. Try and hold on. *Decide to want to look at Me.*

I lead you forward to Heaven. My little one, I remind you you're so little. I need to remind you of My warmth and loving smiles over your day. Let My Mantle, which I have asked you to hold on to, protect you from drifting out of yourself and forgetting Me. Please hold on!"

"I am so often beside you."

Apr. 15–"Hello My sweet little one. Welcome! I endear Myself to you. Don't I? Tell Me you need Me and I will be ever so full of joy. It shall be a joy for Me to stay with you. You gladden My Heart so much My dear child, just because you are little.

I am asking that you, with great trust, hold to our little chats. They will lead to My special graces for you. My sweet little one, where do you find a more comfortable place than in My presence? The days are not long enough for Me to show you how much I enjoy your company.

Even though the Cross looms large in your life, this should give you great consolation that My Son allows you to walk close to Him in His suffering. Do you think I would leave you even for a moment? I am with you so much you don't notice? *I am so often beside you.* My dear child, pray! Let Me hear and see you look at Me as I look at you. Isn't this really why you are so attracted to Me? My simplicity!"

"Be with Me in these thoughts."

Apr. 16–"Hello My dear child. God is calling you to be His little friend. Pray that you respond.

I am helping you to grow in My little chats with you. Don't you feel your life lifted, as it were, to a new awareness of God and Me. Do you?

My little one, pray. You must never allow dryness or any distraction cut you off from Me. My child, I have been with you in a special way.

I invite you to *be with Me in these thoughts* that you stay close and respond to My messages. give you grace through them."

"Please be patient with Me."

Apr. 17–"Hello My sweet little child. You notice I allow you so much to be yourself that I do not take you away from the things you enjoy. But soon I will invite you to hand even these things over to Me. You understand?

My little one, I have been so patient with you. *Please be patient with Me.* My dear child, I am so sweet to you. It all seems so wonderful, too great for you.

Pray. Trust Me. Pray. Believe Me. Pray. I am real. Pray!"

"Be available to My every impulse."

Apr. 18–"Hello My child. I thank you for your fidelity to Me in coming when I call you.

To be in union with whatever My wishes are is My request of you, and that your life be under constant conversion with Me and My Son.

Yes! I know what you are thinking. Don't worry It's not your imagination.

My dear little one, *be available to My every impulse* at this time, that way you will remain near to My Son."

*"To you and eventually everyone will
My Message of Mercy reach."*

Apr. 19–"Hello My little one. Bring all your little odours which you find unpleasant in you and place them at My feet. There I shall ask God to give them a freshness that you may walk closer to Me. My child, light the candle anew every day, if you wish to stay green and full of sap.

Pray that you comprehend My mercy to you, My little one. You forget it is a great grace that enables you to write that which I give you. *To you, and eventually everyone, will My Message of Mercy reach.* Pray that you correspond with Me and keep on writing, even if you don't feel you want to.

Pray about everything - everything - making sure you cast all your cares upon My Heart. I bless you. Peace and love. Thank you for your fidelity in coming when I call."

*"You are, without thought, willing
for all the wrong things."*

Apr. 21–"My little one. The reason you are still so full of fear about your future, is because you are still not ready to hand over, like a child, your life to Me.

You are, without thought, willing for all the wrong things."

"Hold up to Me everything."

Apr. 21–"Hello My poor little one. *Hold up to Me everything* that causes you to keep your heart away from Me. You must act deliberately in letting Me take you away from this world's anxieties.

Pray with Me! Hold on to Me! Think of Heaven and look at Me!

My child, if you want to know My Heart, you must pray, otherwise you will not comprehend the gift I give you. Thank you for your fidelity to Me."

"Do not become heavy with the weight of this world's burden for things."

Apr. 22–"Hello My little one. I am your sweet Mother. I invite you to be very sincere when you are with Me. I invite you to stay with Me. This should give you joy. Do not think of how you should live. Live My child, under My protection.

Can anyone give you more than you could ever have without Me? Let your heart want only the treasure of Heaven. Think often of how I bless you and keep you safe. My little one, be on such a plane that you perceive My special love with you wherever you are.

Do not become heavy with the weight of this world's burden for things. I am all you need. Pray with Me!"

"Listen to My messages."

Apr. 23–"Hello My little one. How much you need Me, poor little instrument. I give you My Maternal love so that you can continue on your way to Me and My Son.

My little one pray for everyone. I invite you ask My help even in trivial things during your day. I am your Mother and so you need to *listen to My messages* of mercy.

Your joy will overflow much more if you receive them with love. Thank you for coming."

"I am looking at you now and smiling."

Apr. 23–I said *'I miss you terribly.'*

"My sweet little one, take My Heart and you won't be alone. So cosy! Would you not find a more loveable heart than Mine? You should try to escape often from yourself to My Heart.

My child, try and be closer to Me than you were yesterday. Oh My little one, give Me your little impoverishment. I am rich in grace. I will fill you up. My little one do you know this? *I am looking at you now and smiling.* Isn't this a beautiful thought? Hold on to it lest you fail to catch it's lightness. Reflect on this.

Don't I give you such special attention, My poor little one? Is this not a mark of My special love for you? Can you still find space to doubt My little tender moments with you?"

"What can I say if you don't pray?"

Apr. 24–"My little one. Prayer! Prayer! *What can I say if you don't pray?* From your heart I wish to exhort you, pray! I cannot stress the importance.

My little one, bring Me your sorrow, all your troubles even your temptations, then I can help you overcome them. Do you understand? Do you understand?

My little child, you will have visitors. Open your heart to them. Pray that they have a good stay. Help them. Pray for them.

My child, you sometimes don't want to do what I tell you. You are stubborn. Help Me remove this obstacle from your heart. Prayer! Prayer! This is the only means you have.

I stay with you. I am good to you. Return your love by inviting Me into your heart. Thank you for coming, My child."

*"I am your Mother, this is why
I stay with you."*

Apr. 25–"My child, you wonder why I come in this way. Is it not the smallest and weakest of a family that needs the most attention? You must believe you are the one I have chosen to write, weak doubtless you are, My *Message of Mercy to the World.*

My child, God wants you to know that life is short and that you were meant for Eternity. My child, don't worry. You are especially chosen but you won't understand everything of what I am doing. Only in Heaven will you realise all.

Pray. Thank God for this grace. I bless you and do really come. *I am your Mother, this is why I stay with you.* I will never abandon you. Thank you for your fidelity."

"You need Me."

Apr. 26–"Hello My child. You, like so many, take My love for granted, but when things go wrong you are there with your petitions.

Please, My child, I do not want to have to tell you, *you need Me* in good and bad times, now more than ever when Satan is redoubling his efforts to destroy you and all that I am doing for you."

"You forget I am your little rudder."

Apr. 27–"Hello My little one. I come to you fresh as a morning flower. Let My voice melt your heart and blossom under My loving glance.

You are so taken up by this or that duty and *you forget I am your little rudder,* who should guide you and bless each duty you undertake.

Remember, My sweet little one, you have a real mother in Me. I help you move through the trials of each day with peace and calm. Did you notice? My little one, like the new pod, spring up under My help, and don't try and rush My maternal touch in your life.

Let Me do everything in My time. Thank you for coming!"

"I won't leave you."

Apr. 28–"Hello My little one. I give you joy when I come. This is to keep you close to all I am doing here. Don't be afraid. *I won't leave you.* I am with you every day. Please be aware of this.

My little one, if you do not see Me at work it is because you fail to quicken your desire for Heaven. This is why I stay so long with you, to help you realise that I want you in Heaven with Me.

My child, pray with faith. Let it penetrate your life in all you do. This is how you should be, My little child, letting Me do everything for you. Thank you for your fidelity."

"Pray slowly! Take time to pray."

Apr. 29–"My dear child, I should be sad with you when you are impatient with things. I am a Mother and I look at you and smile. *Pray slowly! Take time to pray.* You are My little child and I want you to be sweet when you pray, so think of only pleasing Me.

My little one, don't be always thinking *'What am I doing here?'* If you really want to love Me, do not let any such thoughts trouble you. I invite you, move everything that troubles you out of your soul and invite Me in.

My child, to be holy is to be quiet within, no matter the storm outside. But you must pray to comprehend this gift God is giving you. Thank you for coming."

"I am here to receive all of your requests."

Apr. 30–"Hello My little one. Don't be afraid to call on Me at any time. *I am here to receive all of your requests,* but I cannot give you what you ask if you do not pray.

My child, I hold in My hands grace for you, but you do not respond in the way I want, therefore it goes to waste.

My child, ask God to give you strength to stay with Me at this time, because there are many traps Satan is laying for you. Pray! Thank you for coming."

"Only through the Rosary will you make Me happy."

May 3–"My little one, pray and look to Me for everything. I will not disappoint you. Being ready to accept whatever God sends you is a grace. Pray for this grace!

Only through the Rosary will you make Me happy and keep Satan from the door of your heart.

I am always thinking of new ways to show you that My love is real and that I do let you hear and write down My messages of mercy. Think again on them. Let them be a reminder to you of My love. It is to you I give them.

You think this grace is only reserved for those in enclosed orders. My little one, the precious little tulips I give you are scented with Heaven and will stir you on in virtue. Pray!"

"God is asking of you a total commitment to Me."

May 5–"My little one, take all that I give you and ponder it in your heart. This shall be meat for you. This shall sustain you and keep you safe in My arms. My sweet child, remember that nothing will give you greater joy than being with Me and My Son, Jesus.

God is asking of you a total commitment to Me. Entrust your heart to My special care.

Prayer is like water, it helps your soul become more beautiful. My child, My Son Jesus is looking at you. He wants to draw you closer and is giving you His special graces.

My child, stay little. Even if the world discards you it is of no consequence. I love you and cradle you as My very own."

"I also bless each one of your little duties."

May 6–"Hello My sweet child, I am very happy with you. You bring Me flowers of joy and I give them to My Son.

I also bless each one of your little duties. Don't think they are too little for Me. They are not, and I would want you even if you had no duties to perform.

My child, don't think bad of life's little ups and downs. Where there is the cross you can be sure there is joy. Do you understand? Pray! Thank you. Out of simple desires come blossoms of holiness.

I come with all My plenitude. Seek to avail of My treasures. Seek Heaven where you will be happy. Thank you for coming!"

"You need not worry about anything."

May 7–"My child, God is asking you to want what I want and not what the world offers you.

You separate Me from you if you worry unnecessarily about whether you have everything under control. Why? Have I not told you that *you need not worry about anything* but hold on to Me. My sweet little one, let your day be filled with thoughts of Me smiling at you. This is how you should think.

I am the one who holds your future. Thank you for coming."

"Learn to enjoy all that God gives you."

May 8–"Hello My child. Only in My Heart will you be safe. I lead you back to Me whenever you fall. I give you My grace. My little one, listen to Me with openness. I sometimes leave you to show you how much you should depend on Me.

My child, look at the new growth, the flowers, the blue skies. *Learn to enjoy all that God gives you* and don't be always looking on the cold side. You have Me and My love. Let My hand guide you.

I invite you to always a new spring in your heart where Jesus may take loving walks and be delighted by your charm and beauty. Let Me cultivate your soul. Thank you for coming."

"Thank you for your fidelity."

May 9–"Hello My little one. Even if you have all the trials and are weighed down to the ground and you think nothing can lift you out, one look from Me would raise you instantly out of all your difficulties, My child. So you see I have so much watched over you. I allow no harm come to you.

Is it not a beautiful thing I am doing for you in coming to you like this? Tell Me! Talk about it to Me. Remind your soul of the peace I give it. Hold on to it.

My child, you are so full of little weaknesses. I am compelled to wrap you under My Mantle for fear you might be blown away by the least trial. You understand? Poor little one! *Thank you for your fidelity.*"

"Read Me again. There is layer upon layer for you to digest."

May 14—"My child, hold on to what I have given you. *Read Me again. There is layer upon layer for you to digest.*

My little one, follow all My little wants for you in your life. You are calling Me too little these days so I am left out of so many of your moments. I wish to be part at least of every moment with you. Do not take all for yourself. Leave a part for Me in you. You understand?

Nothing is of use to you without Me in it. If I am not let in, there will be no joy in it for you, only sadness. My poor little one, it is in doing everything with Me you will overflow with joy. Thank you for coming."

"But I love you still."

May 15–"Hello My sweet child. I have so much to give you that I need first for you to ask. If you don't open your little soul to Me, I am left to hold My gifts for you, but they are not held out indefinitely, so please ask for My help.

This is why you sometimes become unaware of My closeness and you think you've made a mistake in thinking I am coming to you. My child, be completely given over to Me, knowing even the little you know about Me. Trust Me! Be prepared to love Me to the end and stand by the little voice.

I know the ugliness of your soul *but I love you still* because you are so little. You think yourself unworthy. You are, but My love is so great, greater than your ugliness. Thank you for coming."

"Be longing always for Me."

May 16–"Hello My child. Come more often to the altar of repose in your heart. There, present the fresh flowers of your love simply to My Son Jesus.

My sweet child, to achieve abandonment you must begin always to *be longing always for Me*, needing Me in all your little moments to talk to Me. Thank you for coming."

"Respond to Me in your heart."

May 17–"Hello My sweet child. You are not misled when you *respond to Me in your heart* in all the little turns I ask you to make in your life. They will lead you to your home with Me.

My child, being here with Me is where you will find strength, only here. Thank you for coming."

"Move within your heart."

May 18–"Hello My child. Weigh the balance of My maternal care against your little worries and you will have no doubt as to the greater.

My child, I am restructuring your life within you, making all ready. My sensitive touch, don't you feel it? Is it not constant? My poor little one, today you could not move because of the rain.

Don't worry. You still only have to *move within your heart* and you are close to Me. Is this not so comforting? Thank you for your fidelity."

"You are only too willing to be misled."

May 19–"Hello My child. Want always to climb higher but slowly, asking Me to help you so that you can comprehend the gift God gives you.

To water My love, you have to hold out your heart. This is My impulse for you, that you give Me the very centre of your heart even to the interior of your soul. My child, pray and I will gladly answer you but only if it fits in with My plan for your life.

Sometimes *you are only too willing to be misled* by Satan. Pray! Hold on to Me. Close the door to him. Thank you for coming."

"I am always here."

May 20–"Hello My little one. Don't be afraid if you are tempted. My grace will help you.

My child, you have in Me a Mother who comforts you in every little area of your day with Me. We are together are we not? Did you not notice? Continue to pray!

I have made you aware of something, that is, to let your heart wander and how to bring it back gently in prayer to Me.

My child, *I am always here*. Never doubt this. Thank you for coming."

"You are safe only in My Heart."

May 21–"Hello My poor little one. You have so many problems I scarcely know where to begin, but I your Mother – you should believe this – have everything under control. See how I have made you aware of My gift! My little one, even the Angels look on with such wonder at what I do for you.

You must be ready to open your heart whenever I call. Like a turtle that invites the waves, only then is it safe! My little one, *you are safe only in My Heart.*"

"I am here even though you do not see Me."

May 21–"*I am here even though you do not see Me. My little one, I see you! Is this not enough and don't I prove My presence by so many little Heavenly messages to you? Is not My voice so sweet as a choir and do you not notice I wait for your invitation?*

My little one, be ever on the crest of My Heavenly inspirations looking always to Heaven for Me as I long with tenderness for your glances.

My child if you wish to be close as I am to you, pray to My Heart. Seek to be wrapped under My Mantle. Think of how I lead you often. Thank you for coming."

"I have you always before My smiling face."

May 22–"Hello My child. Thank you for coming. *I have you always before My smiling face.* This is why at times your soul for no reason is flooded with peace. You see this is how I smile on you.

Today, I granted you a special grace, the grace of knowing how I show you Heavenly longing. It is only when you desire Heaven that you cause My Heart and that of My Son's to leap for joy. Thus I allow you to come very close, so close you almost touched Me!

Pray. Your prayer is so much needed!"

"You can be holy."

May 23–"Thank you for coming. My little one, to be trying to be good is reaching out for Me and Heaven. This is grace at work in your soul. My simplicity is so that you find it easy to listen to My portents of love.

Pray! Trust! Know that *you can be holy* only in My arms. Rely on Me to lead you. Neglecting to render this snatches from you the beauty I hold out to you."

"You should value the time I give you."

May 24–"Hello My child. Did you hear Me call today? My little one, listen to My call every day, the call to holiness, to Me, to rely on Me in every minute corner of your day. This is My gift! My child, you are so near Me.

Don't waste time with the world. *You should value the time I give you* when I come. Cancel out in every detail attachments to creatures My little one, only when you put your trust in Me will you know the way.

My child, reflect Me in your daily work by being docile to every second you have with Me. Bathe totally. Lose yourself totally in Me so as to give all your little desires and wants over to Me.

Every knowing moment when you are aware of Me, make a supplication to My Heart '*I need You, Amen!*' Pray thus and so many of your little fears will disappear. Thank you for coming."

"Did you notice a peace."

May 25–"Hello My child. My poor little one, you understand so little, but because of this your charm becomes more endearing to My Son who draws near you because of your littleness. My little one, the joy you will give to Me will be repaid a hundred times over in Heaven and also to all who take into their hearts My messages.

Are you My little one, still little? If you wish to remain little, then give Me those imperfections that hinder you from being close to My Heart. So much you have to begin to understand but you must pray and it will slowly become clearer, that where your heart is going, there is your joy, My little one. So make sure it is coming to Me and not into the darkness.

I am in light. Be moved to stay in My light because now Satan can also see this light, Me with you. *Did you notice a peace* when you read My messages? This is My gift to all who read them with love. Thank you for your fidelity."

"Continue to pray."

May 26–"Hello My child. I am sad today. My Heart is pierced with the coldness of men. Pray to Our Hearts that My pain be eased.

My child, I warn you! Satan will try and destroy My work and all I am doing for you. No more will he rest until he has totally made useless My plan.

Pray. Hide My messages carefully. Their wonder has been seen by him now. My child, I will not come for the next three days. Please do not abandon your visits because of this but *continue to pray*. Thank you for coming."

"Do not abandon the Rosary."

May 30–"Thank you, My child, for coming. You warm My Heart when you respond to My call. This is My call, that you love Me and My Son with all of your heart for the conversion of the world.

This, My child, is why I come, to ask as one in need of alms for My poor children! My little one, behold My Heart pouring forth special graces for you. Let this Heart be your only refuge.

My little one, I am glad you did not become discouraged for the time I did not come but you held out to Me your heart expectantly. This is what helps you grow more and more and gives you greater light so that you learn to trust Me.

Pray. *Do not abandon the Rosary*. It's the holiest of My jewels. Let it penetrate into your soul."

"Hand over to Me everything."

May 31–"Hello My child. Think often of how My maternal care causes you to yearn for Heaven with Me. Let the sun of God's love shine into your heart. Allow Him to open you to the ways of infinite holiness. You can't seek a greater than Heaven. What in the world is greater? Let your soul have full reign as to what is true and eternal. Only then will you know My presence and be aware of what I am doing.

My dear little one, don't let your desires get in the way of your lasting joy. Leave and *hand over to Me everything* that you have no control over. These bright, magnificent lights are nothing compared to the light of Heaven.

My child, pray to be released from Earth's hold on you and seek for that which frees you so that you may open to Me. Pray!"

"Don't be offended if God sends you trials."

June 2–"My dear little one, bring Me every little fly that annoys you and I will free you from its annoyance. Today, My Son has many graces for you and many little lights for you to enjoy.

Don't be offended if God sends you trials for the interior of your heart, they help! Accept them as you would from a friend trying to heal you.

Little by little is how I invite you from the things that catch your eyes. Don't think I am letting you wander through this world without wanting all of your soul's glances. Don't worry. Let Me hold it for you. I can turn it into a delight for you. Pray!"

"You My child console Me."

June 4–"My child, this is one of My little flowers. Take it and receive it with joy. By your acceptance of this from My hand, you bring My Son glory and make My heavy Heart happy.

My little one, is there any more you need than Me? Don't I care for you as a newly hatched egg? My little dove, pray that only My Heart be pleased in all of your little trials. Listen, they are reminders that eternity awaits.

You, My child, console Me when so many want to enjoy and flit around the pleasures of this world not thinking of the next. My dear child, don't worry. I hold you and caress you close to My Heart. This is a special grace! Rest on My Heart today."

*"Thank you for the patience
with your cross."*

June 5–"My child, pray many Rosaries. Today, too few pray My Rosary. The Church is falling because of this.

My little one, love Me with all of your heart. Offer Me many little sacrifices – even the smallest count. *Thank you for the patience with your cross* I sent you.

Give Me all your smiles during these sad times. My Heart is heavy. Pray."

"My Immaculate Heart is very sad."

June 6–"My child, write with a heavy heart these words I shall give you today.

My Immaculate Heart is very sad. Pray! Pray!

My little one, do you know it is My love that sustains you and it is My strength that has held you during your cross. Trust Me more."

"I do everything."

June 7–"My child, please pray when you feel like this. These little moments of frustration are sent to help you overcome your little imperfections.

I got you to make for Me an offering of your little worries today. So many times you don't think I can do this. *I do everything.* For every stain you cause, I make clean and give it back to God. How beautiful!

I invite you to suspend your decisions on anything you might be planning. I am going to reorganise your plans and change direction. Don't be alarmed. It will be only minor surgery.

Please pray for the world that another war may be avoided. Thank you for coming."

> *"Ponder in your heart all that
> I am doing there."*

June 8–"Hello My little one. Let every one of your heartbeats remind you of My constant attention to you.

My poor child, so changeable as the weathercock. When will you stay long enough to be able to really *ponder in your heart all that I am doing there?*

So, what have I to do to make you understand distractions are your lot in this valley of tears and even being repugnant to yourself is the plate at your door. Don't mind to say this is so heavy. It is, but My help will see you through. This is all you need. I bless you, poor child."

"Be on guard not to parade your brightness."

June 9–"Hello My child. Bright and clean is the way I would have your soul. This is how you should look before My Son. But still I have so many corners – yet you do not allow Me enter. I ask you to give Me every little patch of your soul. I wish to cultivate it and make it beautiful for God, hidden to the world.

Be on guard not to parade your brightness before men, lest you become smug and complacent and thus remain in a state of illusion!

I am greatly pleased when you want Me to help you and you no longer rely on your own merits but mine to give your soul a lustre, so that before God you will look beautiful.

My child, so many flowers have yet to be planted. Set the ground by your prayer and fidelity to Me. I bless you."

"I give you all you need."

June 10–"My little one, *I give you all you need*. I nourish you with My Son's Body and Blood. I remove sin with the help of My grace in Confession.

I invite you to pray and hear Mass as often as you can.

I hold you up when you are weak. Is there any more I can do for you that I haven't already done, so please let Me do all!

Just seek to please Me and you will find Heaven."

"Pray for My intentions."

June 11–"My child, My Immaculate Heart bleeds for men. It wants to wrap all of My poor in its furnace. *Pray for My intentions!*

My little one, you have been entrusted with a special mission to bring My *Message of Mercy* to everyone – to the Priests, to the sick, to the sinners, to the savants of error to lead them back to Me, but later on. What I need now is your prayer and fidelity to Me.

Hold on to My beautiful beads. Pray them with love and allow the graces of each mystery penetrate your life.

My child, I can't let My Heart unless you ask for a room there. Please, I invite lovingly you to come here. You will be safe. Pray. Peace."

"Remain sweet and beautiful."

June 11–"Hello My little one. Remain on My Heart. Cling to every impulse of its love. Notice every ray of light I give you to help you overcome all temptation.

My sweet! this is how you *remain sweet and beautiful* by your closeness to Me, by letting Me guide your heart in every one of its thoughts. My child, I direct your soul to see clearly and be bright and clean."

"I shall protect you."

June 13–"My child, I announce to you that My Immaculate Heart is too much offended and I invite you to pray for grace to overcome all of your temptations.

My child, I have led you to My Immaculate Heart where you may find repose. You cannot be hurt while you repose on My Heart. *I shall protect you from every kind of attack.*

This, you should know is My secret, that My Immaculate Heart will lead you to Heaven."

"Pray for poor sinners."

June 16—"My child, I look upon you as one close to My Heart. To you I allow so much. Is this not tenderness from a sweet Mother?

My child, *pray for poor sinners* who need so much to know of God's mercy towards them. Help Me realise all I must complete. It is on prayer and your love for Me that so much is restored!

This is something you must pray about because God is giving you His blessing these days. Avail of it by your openness to Me. Then I can give you more."

"Melt under My touch."

June 17–"My little one, thank you for coming. Your heart should be constantly looking at Me, then I can shower you with special flowers.

My child be like the wax on a candle burning before My Son. *Melt under My touch* then I can mould you with ease.

Throw away thoughts of every kind that stays you to earth. Rise above them and want Me to be near. I am! You see I let you come very close."

"Pray about everything."

June 18–*'O Mary help me!'*
"My child, I do help you! I help you more times than you turn your heart to Me. I have to invite you often to come and I look at you with love, thus I draw you closer.

My child, pray before you look at My messages. Of course I will give you light but you must invoke Me.

This is so rare! You should thank God for His providence. Let Him send you what He wills. Accept with faith and *pray about everything.*"

"I promise to give special graces."

June 20–"Hello My child! Today I look upon you and smile. I think of how I can help you blossom under My constant care. By so many graces do I draw you and give you hope so that you don't become discouraged.

My child, *I promise to give special graces* to everyone who looks to Me and reads My *Message of Mercy* with hope. Thank you for your fidelity."

"I give you My blessing."

June 21–"My child, don't scold yourself. I embrace you when you think you are not so pure. I approach and cover you with My Mantle. My child, you don't yet perceive what I give you.

Pray more with the heart, then you become beautiful and fresh. I give to you My special peace. Pray with faith! Come with love in your heart!

Don't let little flies alter your course, the course I have set for you. *I give you My blessing.*"

"I have taken it into My Heart."

June 22–"My little one, don't bring your past around with you. *I have taken it into My Heart,* there, like everything, it is wrapped up in Me and thus beautified so that you may not trouble yourself about it any more.

If you are made aware by some malediction of Satan, close the door gently and ask to be rescued by Me.

My child, even if you were as weak as you are, I can, with My touch, bring to without trouble your sanctity, but Divine Providence has willed that you stay like the hen on the ground. Come, My little one, even slowly, I will help you come."

"Take some one of My thoughts around with you."

June 25–"Hello My child. I am asking that you give Me some little token of your affection and ask Me to remind you to present it to Me in your heart.

Also I ask that you *take some one of My thoughts around with you* each day. That way I am ever close and you don't forget to call on Me in your heart. This! It may seem strange at first but, if you persevere, great graces will be bestowed upon you. My hand has been so generous with gifts for you. Ask, seek and they will multiply."

"Special favours will be granted."

June 26–"*Special favours will be granted,* My child, if you sing with love this Hymn in your heart – *'O Virgin, defend me all pure and sweet.'*"

* See Hymn Page 612

"In all difficulties pray, pray, pray."

June 26–"Hello My little one. Bless them that harm you and cause you interior trials.

I have much that you must yearn for. Don't waste time speculating as to what the future and how everything will turn out. All you need know is that *in all difficulties pray, pray, pray!*"

"Hold on to My most Holy Rosary."

July 1–"Hello My child. Perilous times await the Church and especially the Poor and Consecrated! My child, hold fast to Me even though persecution is on every side!

Hold on to My most Holy Rosary and stay under My Mantle, that is, close to all I give you.

My child, you will experience changes in your soul because of My messages. These are the fruits. Don't be alarmed! They bring you peace and will comfort you in the times when you are sad."

"Let My messages sink in."

July 2–"Hello My child. I guide you through the darkness of this world to the light of Heaven. My child, don't worry whether it's true or not. I tell you, it's Me! Can I not come in the manner I wish, to any mere mortal?

My little one, take a new look at what I am doing for you. *Let My messages sink in.* They will enlighten your soul. Tell the one who has charge of your soul all about what I am doing, simply and with confidence.

My child, pray. Ask God to help you in this. It is for Him. This should help you bear all."

"Pray about all I have given you."

July 3–"Hello My child. I smile at you often. My glances are full of sweetness, are they not? My child, I have been with you a long time. You have received My counsels with love. I thank you for this.

Now I invite you to *pray about all I have given you* and be obedient to My love, then you cannot be harmed by Satan."

"Let Me calm every storm."

July 4–"Hello My child. I always wait for you. I am the one who calls you and helps you pray, otherwise you would have given up long before.

My child, I can see your soul, thus you may understand why I do not deal with you as you think in human terms, as the world. Place your heart upon mine. You are never left wanting if you do.

So many of My poor children are burdened by every kind of oppression. How I wish to heal them and thus lift their burdens. My child, if you are inconsolable, it is because you do not hold out to Me your little self in each of your trials, thus you are more tired and left exhausted.

My child, *let Me calm every storm* for you, thus you remain little. I know how to deal with all of the problems of this world. Do you understand? Pray."

"Begin anew!"

July 6–"Hello My little one. Pray in your soul and you won't feel so heavy the trials of this life. I know how you are and how you find it all.

Begin anew! Every time you look at Me, I will help you. My child, so little! I am so happy with you.

This is My delight to see you totally abandoned to Me, then you feel bankrupt and I am the one who consoles. Pray!"

"Don't worry! Pray."

July 7–"Hello My poor little one, so afraid of everything, of even failing to invite Me in when you know that I love to be asked.

My little one, don't be like the grasshopper who can't wait to explore the next leaf. Trust it to Me. I know what I will give you but it is only for you to write. You see I help you even in this.

My child, the world is closing in on My little instrument, but My Immaculate Heart will protect and see to it that all is as it should be.

Don't worry. Pray the Rosary with love in your heart."

"Do not be afraid of being small."

July 8–"Hello My child. Use every opportunity to send little love glances to Me so as I can use them for whatever I may.

My child, *do not be afraid of being small*. I hold you all the more and God blesses you. My little one, you are so taken with this or that duty that I am left out so much these days.

Remind yourself I am looking at you and hoping for some turn of your heart, thus I can transform your moment. Pray."

"Don't pray with sadness in your soul."

July 11–"Hello My child. I invite you. Come with Me in your heart to My Son and give Him all your anxieties, and He will give you His grace and make your heart leap for joy.

My little one, *don't pray with sadness in your soul*. By doing this you are making God sad.

Give Me every tiny look that you would give to everything around you when you come to Mass thus God can illuminate your heart. Pray. Pray. Pray."

*"Listen always to Me and you will find
the path that leads to peace."*

July 14—"Hello My poor little one. This world should hold out nothing for you. It has only that which will drag your soul down.

I, your Blessed Mother, am protecting you from compromising with everything this world has to offer you, so please *listen always to Me and you will find the path that leads to peace.* Pray. Pray. Pray."

"The Mother of God knows best."

July 14–My Guardian Angel :---
 'The Mother of God knows best.'
 "This prayer will help you to do God's will."

"Hello My little one."

July 14–*"Hello My little one.* Tell (…) that My Immaculate Heart will be her refuge."

"Patience! My love will guide you."

July 15–"Hello My child. *Patience! My love will guide you.*"

"I know all about your faults!"

July 17–"Hello My little one. Do you not yet know I am looking after everything and that I help you spend each moment in My company?

My child, did it not seem to you that My love should not encircle every corner of your day, even those you do not think you are disposing by your forgetfulness of Me.?

My child, do not think I am not near even though you look within and find only your faults. *I know all about your faults!* Throw them away the moment you think of them and look at Me and all will be well. All will be well."

"I am the one who leads you."

July 19–"My dear little one, I am pleased with you even though your heart can be in turmoil at times. Do not worry about this.

I am the one who leads you. My dear child, when I come I am giving you My love and asking God to help you in a special way. Peace."

*"I hold you more secure
than you think."*

July 19–"My dear child, *I hold you more secure than you think*. I, your Mother, am pushing back all that would draw you away from Me. I know best how to lead to God.

My child, even though it seems dark and you don't know yet which way I am leading, My hand guides you safely. This is all you need know."

"Please hold on to My Rosary."

July 20–"Hello My dear little one. Today so much grace is poured among people and so much is wasted that God is sad that so few respond.

Blossom like the poor flower that you are, under God's goodness, then I can bring you along the path I have planned for you with greater certainty.

Please hold on to My Rosary and pray that all I am doing may bear fruit. Peace! Peace!

I ask that you come every day to Me so as you may be strengthened, then I can make sure of My purpose."

"My plan is in its final stages."

July 21–"Hello My child! Be on guard against being dulled by My seemingly normality of My rendezvous with you. Take not My silence as some reproof of you.

I don't want to break this time I have with you however casual it may all seem. This is so as you write simply My message, without any foreign interference.

Satan is trying to discourage these meetings by methods which, if you stay here and are faithful, will have no effect. Thus I shall render his diabolical useless.

My child, it is near to the end. *My plan is in its final stages* but for you it is only beginning so don't think I will leave you. Oh no! I am your Mother and I shall continue to talk with you daily. Pray."

*"I am announcing to the world
not a new message."*

July 22–"These messages I give are not for you alone, but for all who may come so that they too see the light even though they be in a dark place.

My child, *I am announcing to the world not a new message* but a message that will make men new. Pray! Pray! Pray!"

*"I know how slow it all must be
but God will not be rushed."*

July 24–"My child, *I know how slow it all must be but God will not be rushed* and it is for you to wait and pray that this – which He allows – that is, Me to stay with you, continue even though you sometimes are so uneasy about it all.

If I don't come, how am I to let you know My *Message of Mercy*? Did I not tell you to hold on to My Mantle because Satan is trying to pull you away?

My child, if you ask God to be near, He will give you His deep abiding presence so as you therefore may rest more with patience in My arms and everyone will see God in you!"

"I don't want you worrying."

July 26–"My child, *I don't want you worrying* about your little weaknesses. Leave them in My Heart and trust Me to take care of all.

The way I would want you is to be abandoned and not trying to do that which you know nothing about, namely Heaven! Only with Me and with prayer will you come to your home so don't worry.

I ask that you accept My love and don't block it by your ongoing retention of trying to be perfect. Let Me take care of this. Are you not under My Mantle and don't I see to it that your soul though weak is never left in despair? My child, this is why you should not be afraid. Simply do as I tell you.

Remain you will, poor, before Me always. It is not to hinder you that I ask that you stay poor before Me. I ask this so as therefore My Son may be glorified. Pray! Pray! Pray!"

"I invite you to look at My Heart."

July 28–"Hello My little one. *I invite you to look at My Heart*. Go there! I point to My most Holy Rosary.

My child, if you are tired, then be at once ready to pray in My Heart, then you won't be so tired. I have very much in addition to what I have already given for you, so remain on under My loving gaze.

You do this by going to pray My Rosary. Here is the fountain! drink and refresh yourself. By means of this Holy Rosary I will lead you to Heaven."

"Pay attention to My messages."

July 30–"My child, you must hold on to Me if God is to give you His blessing. I invite you to more being in My Heart and letting Me guide you. I don't want you doing everything with a reckless abandon.

Pay attention to My messages. I invite you. Be led on the way of gentleness, kindness and helping everyone as I then am with you."

"I am asking for your help."

July 31–"My dear little one. Look well at this poor shrine I have led you to. It resembles the hearts of men. See! Behold the Cross. It stands alone amid such indifference.

God cannot hold back any longer His Hand at such slumber towards My Crucified Son who bleeds for such who only show Him for the most part their indifference.

My child, look at Me! I am offering My Son, His peace to men. Place your littleness at the foot of the Cross, then I am therefore able to gain for you such that will lead poor ignorant men back to God. Pray!

I am asking for your help. This is where I invite you to come from now on."

"I do smile with mercy on you."

Aug. 3–"Hello My little one. See how I bring you to My feet even though you think you have no right. The proud and powerful of this world think like this. They allow only those whom they think worthy should approach My Son, but it is to the small and little that My Son asks to come to My feet. This is why you are not afraid anymore.

This, My child, is a special grace I have given you. I have let you perceive My Heart. My little one, don't you feel warm? Isn't this everything and even more than you could have imagined? Oh how I thank God for this which He allows Me, this time when I come to bless you with My presence.

I am here, you don't see Me. You are now as I wish you to be, little, even now in My arms I am loving you and *I do smile with mercy on you.*

"Come to Me in trust."

Aug. 3–"Hello My child. You have now very few doubts. This is Me helping you come. *Come to Me in trust.*"

"Those that trust Me, God will bless."

Aug. 4–"Hello My child. Did you notice My peace which you received when I was with you today? Just as you continue to come so do I give you My Heart. *Those that trust Me, God will bless.* My child, you are My little one! My love has you so well wrapped up, you find it easy to pray.

Don't be in fear about the cross you carry, I help you bear it with love! Now I invite you to come to Me, not with a heavy heart, by this you become tired and you find all so difficult to bear. I give you Jesus who knows what you feel.

Don't be afraid of your faults. Offer them to Me with simplicity and you help sinners repent. Pray. Pray. I bless you."

"Don't grow weary of loving those whom you are with everyday."

Aug. 8–"Dear little one. I invite all to come to My Son in the Tabernacle. Love Him there where He is most insulted and left abandoned.

To you, I am letting you come close to Heaven. You do when you come to receive My message each day.

Dear child, *don't grow weary of loving those whom your are with everyday.* I help you in this so be always ready to open your heart to all, thus I can convert. I thank you for your love. I bless you. Go in peace."

*"Leave everything in obedience
to your Confessor."*

Aug. 10–"Hello My dear child. I wish to make known certain things. But first you must never tell, only those whom I let you. My dear child, God wishes to draw souls in great numbers through this *Message of Mercy* thus His Mercy may more abundantly spread.

First, My dear child, tell the one in charge of your soul to have this message made known to whom he sees fit so as to better help Me.

My dear child, the time has come when I must act. It is only for you to pray. *Leave everything in obedience to your Confessor.*"

"Pray that you leave everything in My hands."

Aug. 12–"My dear child, *pray that you leave everything in My hands* thus you will receive God's peace. My hand is guiding you.

Look not to other things to give you peace. They will only leave you sad. It is by God's love that you be strengthened.

My Heart is helping you come closer to My Son, Jesus, who prepares you to receive great graces.

Pray for all Religious who are bowed down. I bless you. Pray!"

*"Bring Me all the little worries
of each day.*

Aug. 13–"Hello My child. You are surprised. Yes. I am talking to you so late. *Bring Me all the little worries of each day.* And while just before you go to sleep, thank My Son for His loving care that He sends Me to give you comfort.

Pray! Am I not always the one who asks? Do you need anymore than Me? Don't I carefully hide you under My Holy Mantle? Is it not the sweetest place to be, close beside Me? Don't you feel so warm with Me?

I bless you. Peace! Peace! Peace!"

"Pray for poor sinners."

Aug. 13–"My dear child. Just as you listen and hear My messages, just as you come to know My closeness, so too many of My little ones will take delight in reading My messages.

They point to the Heart of your Mother who looks down on Her poor children with sadness and eyes filled with tears because so many have left Jesus to die alone.

My child, write, write, My child to them. They are breaking your Mother's Heart who can't but cry for them, Her poor children. My child, you are invited to such that you feel somewhat the agony of My Son and My tears which fall in vain.

Pray for poor sinners. Pray! I bless you."

"Do not fear anything."

Aug. 14–"My dear child, I hold you. *Do not fear anything,* for My love embraces even your most severe temptations to despair.

Can a moth fail to be drawn by the lamp of even the smallest kind? It does not hinder it because it is the darkness that accentuates the lamp's brightness. So too are you not that fearful, but still you are drawn by My light in this dark world.

Don't think just because My light seems so small compared with your fear of things, thus you think *'How will it survive?'* Dear child, My hand is quite happy to guide and quite capable of leading you through any fear.

Dear child, simply open to Me. Pray! I bless you."

"All you need do is pray."

Aug. 15–"Dear child, pray that you let Me do with you as I wish therefore you set in motion, My little one, so much. *All you need do is pray* and respond to Me.

Dear child, you are My little instrument that will pass on to everyone My *Message of Mercy,* thus My Son, Jesus, may live among men. Pray! Don't be afraid to receive My message. It has so much to accomplish even yet. I see so many who would try to see what I am doing here destroyed by so many ways. God is protecting My message thus it is still hidden from the world.

Dear little one, I invite you. Continue with confidence in Me. I am leaving you with this gift of Me with you. Don't worry about your heart, you really hear Me, it is no illusion. I bless you. Pray! Pray! Pray!"

"I shall comfort you Myself."

Aug. 15–"My dear child, I hold out to you My Immaculate Heart. Come! Take refuge here. I invite you here whenever you feel lost or lonely. I promise *I shall comfort you Myself* and give you My special love.

Do not become so distracted by this or that, that you forget Me there in your midst. My dear little one, I love you so much. Don't think I could ever abandon you.

Come to Me full of joy. My love will see to it that you do not become discouraged. I thank you, dear child, for your fidelity. Peace."

"I care for you."

Aug. 16–"Dear child. I am giving you the warmest smiles these days, thus you don't feel so over troubled about your cross. My little one, take My hand. Let Me be the one to lead you. See Me everywhere. I don't want you to be forgetful of how *I care for you.* Pray that you still look with wonder at what I do for you.

Please, I want you to see that My love for you will overturn so much in your life, but don't be alarmed. Be like the bottle-top only waiting to be turned, thus its contents may spill out. You understand? I take every one of your little glances to My Heart. You think, sometimes I forget to look at you. You think I am too busy. My child, I see right into your heart.

Are you not My child? Are not all a gardener's flowers precious to him? Is it not so with Me? Remember you are always in My Heart. I am touching your life every day even if you do not perceive it!

When you make the effort to pray, I respond with so much love that I am so close yet you do not see Me. Know that I am here. Pray with this touching thought in your heart every day. Your prayer comes to Me, thus I receive it with tenderness and render it still sweeter to My Son. Pray. I bless you."

"This is God's work."

Aug. 20–"My child! I have given you the Image which God wishes spread in all homes and those who honour it God will bestow great graces.

God wishes that everyone should come to know the love in My Immaculate Heart.

Show this Image to your Confessor giving him the instruction that *this is God's work* and I shall bless him abundantly if he should accept. Pray! Thank you for coming."

*'Our Lady Queen of the Home,
pray for us.'*

Aug. 20–She reveals the Title:
"Have this inscription at the bottom of My Image."
'Our Lady Queen of the Home, pray for us.'

"Peace be to you."

Aug. 21–"Hello My little one. *Peace be to you.* I thank you for coming where so many have left My Son alone.

My child, your soul is being slowly awakened to the things of Heaven. No more will it long for the clang of earth or the bells of praise but for the sound of wings.

My child let Me lead you above disdain and lead you on the high ground where all is beautiful, where even the sounds of everyday become a symphony.

My child, you are being called to partake of the joys of My Heart, this place where there are green fields of hope, enchanted houses of trust and so much more. Pray. I bless you."

"God permits a new opening."

Aug. 22–"My child, today God wishes to proclaim a new Feast dedicated to the title –
'Our Lady Queen of the Home'.

My child, the Image (Image of Peace) shall be also honoured on this day.

God permits a new opening of My Heart on all who honour My Image on this day. Pray I bless you."

"It will be like a fresh breeze."

Aug. 23—Our Lady has told me to write in my own words explaining the Novena. She told me it starts on the *Eve of the Assumption* and ends on the *Queenship of Mary* and also *Our Lady Queen of the Home*.

The Chaplet itself is as follows:-
Creed, Our Father, Hail Mary, Glory be-

On the large beads:
O Virgin defend me, all pure and sweet.   3 times

On the small beads:
Our Lady Queen of the Home, pray for us.

At the end:
The Hail Holy Queen.
She asks to pray this Chaplet once a day during the Novena.

She said also, "*it will be like a fresh breeze* blowing through the Church."

"Don't worry about anything."

Aug. 23–"Hello My little one! *Don't worry about anything*. My grace will help. Is there any more you need?

My child, pray with confidence. My Son accepts your prayers when you give them to Me. Pray! Pray! Pray!"

"Place all your heartache in My care."

Aug. 24–"Hello My little one! *Place all your heartache in My care* and don't put particular attention on troubles that have little worth. Pray. Respond. I bless you."

"Pray. I am smiling at you."

Aug. 25–"Hello My poor little one. You are on so many wavelengths, you do not prepare for when I come.

Don't be letting the world's distractions home in on you. Stay at the one point in your soul then it won't wander. *Pray. I am smiling at you.*"

"This is a precious flower."

Aug. 26–"Hello My little one. I hope you are not too sad with the way things have been. God is blessing you and thanks you for your love. My Heart holds you close and My care is, I know, so hidden these days, just as though I were not here.

This is a precious flower Jesus sends you, this emptiness, thus you are left to grow without the rays of the sun. My child, you are made strong by this process. Even if you fail to see any growth, there is.

I am letting you know this obscurity to help you prepare for the cross God is making ready for you, therefore I want you to rely on Me more.

Refuse to listen to the noise of Satan. Come to Me in your heart where I can form you without any intrusions. Pray! Pray! Pray!"

She just smiles.

Aug. 27–*She just smiles.* She is very beautiful.

"Love makes up for lost effort."

Aug. 28–"Hello My dear child! Simple is the way I would have you, every other way tends to distort. It is in little things, a lot of little things that you fail.

So in these little things must you build in virtue. Therefore, you come to know that God is more pleased in love than in any other way.

This *love makes up for lost effort* and lacking in promptness. I bless you. Continue to come."

"I, My child understand."

Aug. 29–"Hello My dear child. To hold on is to try and be close to Me. So many of My children are being drawn away from Me and those that foster devotion to Me are most persecuted.

The little ways you love Me help them in their suffering. So many need prayer.

My child, it is to you I invite to be My little instrument in opening the Font of My Immaculate Heart so as they may draw there consolation, thus they may not grow weary in their troubles.

I, My child, understand My children and give them My blessing. Pray. Pray. Be at peace."

"God is watching you."

Aug. 30–"My child, even if you are weighed down you are still in My arms. *God is watching you.*

Look to Me for your only comfort in this life. Through Me you will be safe. Through Me you have no better way to Heaven. Pray. Peace."

"Keep My Son company."

Aug. 31–"My child, if you were to sit here and *keep My Son company* for this time everyday, you would be doing God's will and living out your vocation to the full. My child, you are called to write to the world My *Message of Mercy*. Pray! Pray! Pray!"

"Nothing gives Me greater joy."

Aug. 31–"Hello My little one. I am with you so many times. You fail to confide in Me like a child. This is how you should come to Me. Simply tell Me all your troubles. I will listen to them one by one. None are too small for Me.

I am in Heaven but I still want to hear all about your little headaches. I value each little time you come to Me. No, you're never boring to Me. I am so intimately interested in all that happens to you.

You are very close to eternity when you invite Me to your heart. Please, I am your Mother, Maternal guide. Don't think I don't wish to talk with you.

Nothing gives Me greater joy than to have My little children confide in Me. I bless them. I bless you."

"I look with pity on all My children."

Sept. 1–"My poor child, pray that God may be heeded through all that He is doing to help men in their pain.

I look with pity on all My children and ask you to pray with Me for them. I bless you."

"You are so small and weak."

Sept. 2–"Hello! You are so frightened by so many little things. I am holding you.

I am looking after you. Even if you fall I implore Jesus to have mercy because *you are so small and weak*. You need special attention. Should this not calm you - give you peace? Trust Me. I will lead you. Pray! Thank you for responding."

"Know that God allows this."

Sept. 3–"Hello My little one. Sometimes you forget that you are at My feet, the feet of your Mother who waits for you.

Do you *know that God allows this* wonderful thing to happen because others have prayed? Not you. It is not because you are any different. Don't think this. I suppose you don't fully realise just what it means – all this, Me talking to you in such a manner that would shock even the liliest of towers in the Church. But this is to show how humble and caring I am.

I am able just as well to deal with the highest as well as the lowest, thus you are aware you are so relaxed with Me. This is prayer. This is holy. Pray for all who think there is some mysterious way to My Heart and think it cold and distant. Poor little ones. I bless you. Thank you for responding."

"Let Me revive it for you."

Sept 4–"Hello My child. Don't think that all is lost if you feel devotion in your heart is waning. *Let Me revive it for you.* My child, you have still a bit more to go before you are free.

Let Me be the one to be your only consolation, that way you have only Me, and you see how empty all other pleasure is. Trust Me. Pray. I bless you."

"Let My love give you strength."

Sep. 4–"Hello My dear child. I have something rather important to tell you! Where My Image is honoured and placed in esteem, God will spare all who live through the night of trial that is to come! A most striking wonder will My Image perform in souls who look with love at Me.

Upon you, My little one, who are true to Me, I will guard and protect because you over a time have been faithful.

Live with this in your heart and *let My love give you strength* so that you never imagine yourself lost. Pray! I am the Blessed Virgin who has revealed this to you."

"Pray with faith!"

Sept. 6 –"Hello My child. Tell (---) I wish her to pray these prayers too, the ones I have given you! My child be patient while all must unfold. *Pray with faith!*

Pray that you remain at My feet thus you will be at peace. Thank you for your fidelity."

"Be still and wait."

Sept. 7–"My child, I know how you are eager to see all I am doing here take off. *Be still and wait on My Maternal hand to guide events, thus all will be accomplished with calm.*

My child, try and look at Me, thus your heart will be at peace no matter how troubled the waters of your earthly life may become.

It is in My Heart (Immaculate Heart) only that you receive this special peace* God is giving the world. Only in Me will you realise all in a special way. Pray. Pray. Pray."

---

* not as the world gives

"Thousands await this Message of Mercy."

Sept. 9–"My child, I called you only to pray. Leave everything to be guided by Me alone. My child, you do not understand fully because it is from above.

This is all you need know that I am protecting you from being struck by Satan. Were you not under My special care, Satan, without hesitation, would destroy you.

Thousands await this Message of Mercy from Me, the Virgin. Pray. Pray. Pray."

"Pray above all for simplicity."

Sept. 10–"Dear little one. Simply do as I invite you along this path full of My sweetness, then you will hear My voice and write down all with My help, without fear of the Evil One. You are with your own thoughts, trying to cure your own problems. It is only by My extraordinary ways will your manifold problems be solved.

Remain close to My *Message of Mercy*, then you will know how to climb the spiritual way I am giving you.

You should *pray above all for simplicity.* There I have said it! This is your calling to be simple.

Every time you want to come close to Me and receive a deluge of grace you must pray. Your spiritual life depends on this if there is to be true conversion. Immediately I call you to pray. Pray, pray, pray."

"Give Me your heart."

Sept. 11–"Hello My little one. Today I invite you in a special way to *give Me your heart*. Then I am truly with you each moment.

There is only one thing that matters, all else is unimportant, and that is to hold on to your belief.

So much damage is done, I'm afraid, by those who do not believe and still come to Church and receive My Son. Pray! I bless you."

'Our Lady's Message of Mercy to the World.'

Sept. 12–Our Lady reveals the title of the diary:
'Our Lady's Message of Mercy to the World.'

"Today I wish you to be wholly Mine."

Sept. 14–"Hello My child. *Today I wish you to be wholly Mine,* therefore I may do with you as I wish. Be My little companion as I show you My Heart and many other things.

My child, do not be distracted! I invite you within, deep into your interior soul, thus you may see and pray with Me for all who do not seek Jesus crucified! My child, let your heart be free! Pray. I am with you."

"Discover My great gentleness."

Sept. 15–"Thank you for coming My child. I wish you to *discover My great gentleness* towards you. You are led to know in your heart that I love you and thus you are quite relaxed in My presence, are you not?

My little one, don't be afraid of Me ever. I am your gentle Mother. I am always gracious with you. Don't you feel My warmth when you come to Me? I am deep in your soul. Look at Me and thank God for allowing Me to come. I am giving you a special grace today. Pray! I bless you."

*"I am calling you to a deeper
awareness of My gift."*

Sept. 16–"Thank you My child. I welcome you every time you come. You have been unaware that God has given you a great grace in your heart by letting Me come. Pray. Let in the light of My presence and in faith live all I am giving you.

Note how *I am calling you to a deeper awareness of My gift.* I wish you to be led by Me. I am with you when you gather in prayer.

Thank God that He allowed you to come across His most precious little gift yesterday. Don't think this just happened. Nothing just happens. God is holding out every moment to you. Don't let Satan take a grip of it from you. Pray! I bless you."

*"Don't forget to invoke your
Guardian Angel."*

Sept. 17–"My child, *don't forget to invoke your Guardian Angel* each night, that way he is delighted to accompany you during your day.

My child, little glances are enough to chase Satan away. Pray! I bless you."

"I have summoned you."

Sept. 18–"My child, now for months, we have been meeting and I have outstretched My arms with graces for you. I have blessed you with My presence, here in this Chapel, which I want especially venerated. Know this, without exception, many know in their hearts that I am visiting them here.

My child, come to My knees and there you will come to know of My many secrets. My child, during these few minutes, special minutes, I have given you an indescribable joy a Mother and Her child.

I have summoned you here My child carefully, where for this time I have entrusted to you My messages. They are in your hands. They must be spread and made known.

To be precise, I see this message being attacked, but I shall defend it Myself. I have made all this known to you. Lose nothing I give you even to the smallest details. Pray. Pray. Pray."

"Believe this extraordinary favour."

Sept. 19–"My child, you are immediately called to preserve in your heart My peace. Many times you fail. Others need your help. Don't think of only yourself. Wear God's armour - Faith, Hope and Love. My child, follow Me in My footsteps, there you will love just as you are called.

I preserve you My child, from the Evil One. I your Mother, have found many thoughts you have corporal. Your life depends on how you think.

Pledge yourself to your Heavenly Mother and offer thus you help others. My child, I am helping you to get to Heaven. For this reason are My words spent on all.

Wear a replica of My Image around your neck. The reason is to protect you from evil. My child just love. I, your Mother, call you in this life to live close to – and *believe this extraordinary favour* of your Immaculate Mother. Pray. I bless you."

---

* The Scapular of Mary Immaculate

"This Message of Mercy is a letter to all."

Sept. 20–"My child I, the Blessed Virgin, wish to pour forth rays of light to My children at My feet. ask you to continue to pray often. Thus you incur much, and help damage all that Satan is doing and bring glory to God.

My child, My Heart is bestowing on the world the wishes of My Son. I wish you to seek Me thus you may not wander through this world blind.

My child, *this Message of Mercy is a letter to all,* especially My Consecrated, thus they may in the world remain immaculate* and preserved by this light. I, your Immaculate Mother, ask you to keep before you My Heart** while you read My letter. Pray. I bless you."

---

* Clean of heart
** The Image

"I am renewing the Church."

Feast of SS. Michael, Gabriel & Raphael, Archangels

Sept. 29–"My dear child! Pray to Michael that he give you his most powerful protection and guide you on to Me safely.

This is a time of special grace for the Church, now that She is entering Her *Anniversary 2000*. God is, through Me, guiding Her to a new splendour.

He will cause Me to shine as never before and all will see how beautiful I am and how I look upon all My children with love.

My child, with Michael *I am renewing the Church* and bringing Her back to new devotion to Me. Pray! Pray! Pray!"

"Open to Me your heart."

Oct. 1–"Hello dear child. If you wish to be able to see more clearly Heavenly things in your life, do this. When you begin to pray, turn your eyes upon an Image of Me and then *open to Me your heart* and wait to receive My grace and then continue to begin praying.

My child, the reason you feel so little devotion is because you are letting too many worldly concerns remain in your heart. If you want to be free of these you must let in the light of My Son and return to a good desire of wanting Me.

My dear child, you are beginning to fall in not opening your heart these days and you become complacent, and I am left with the new flowers which you are not ready to receive. This pains Me to tell you. Try and let My light bring you round and you feel again My sweetness, thus you make Me happy.

I invite you to pray My Rosary with your heart more, then you feel My special presence and I am able to move you. Pray! Pray! Pray!"

"It is never too late to begin to reach depth in prayer."

Oct. 2–"My dear child, I have told you to pray with your heart that you may respond more fully to Me. That way I am able to lead you more easily.

My child, *it is never too late to begin to reach depth in prayer* if you abandon yourself to Me.* Give Me those moments you spend with such impatience that you allow Satan to laugh at you because you do not recognise him.

My child, if you wish to know that you're advancing towards Heaven then look at your heart and how much it gives to Me.

I invite you to really look at Me and pray My Rosary which will lead you on every day. Pray. I am happy. I bless you."

---

* Immaculate Heart of Mary

"Respond I wish you to accept My plea."

Oct. 3–"Dear child, don't be afraid if you are slow to respond.

Give Me your heart, this is what matters. I don't come to let you just be amazed at this when I come. Look at Me and don't be looking for wonders, this is only leading you to emptiness.

I ask that you really please Me by your deep reliance on Me.

My child, if I ask you to *respond, I wish you to accept My plea* and go forward in faith with My peace, the peace I am asking you to hold onto in your heart. I am happy. Thank you for coming. I bless you."

"With prayer, you restore your heart."

Oct. 5–"Dear little one, with food if you are hungry, you restore your strength. So too it is *with prayer, you restore your heart.*"

"You are My dear angel."

Oct. 6–"My dear child. God asks you to be always ready to open your heart to Me. Today I am letting you see that all is not lost when you put your trust in Me. My child, don't be afraid to continue to write My messages.

I am pleased you came today even though the weather is bad. I value all your efforts and God rewards you with special grace. My child, *you are My dear angel.* I, your Mother, love you and hold you close.

Don't be thinking I am sad with you. I am only wanting that you draw close to My Son. Pray. I bless you."

"God will give you light."

Oct. 6–"My child, these days have been weary for you I know, but there is a reason that this is so. You see, your little suffering, if you accept it with love, I am able to help My poor children and *God will give you light* and everything will become clearer for you.

This is how you, My child, are being called. By your abandonment to Me, you open up new doors in your heart and I am able to give you more. I am giving you so much even though you may not see. It's in the depths of your heart.

I ask you please continue to pray your Rosary."

"I call you to remember."

Oct. 7–"Hello My child. *I call you to remember* today in a special way My most Holy Rosary.

This is a most precious prayer to the Father and is a sure means of leading souls to Heaven; also of building up, in faith, My Church on Earth, and uniting souls in a special way to Me.

My little one, you have tasted the sweetness of this prayer in your heart today. This is a grace. I am very much aware that you need to grow more in your heart.

Work in your heart with this most Holy Rosary and God who sees your heart will bless you. Pray! Pray! Pray!"

"All will be well."

Oct. 8–"My child. I love you as you are even though you hurt Me!

I cannot let you go. I am your Mother and I ask that you always ask for grace through Me. This is not so easy when you think you are too disfigured but I am with you.

By My help I wish to open your heart to peace, to seek God and Me more than you did yesterday, and carry on.

My child, I give you My special grace. Accept it from Me. It's yours. Pray. Continue. *All will be well.*"

"Leave everything to God."

Oct. 9–"How are you My child? My child, I am pleased to come. Your heart is not so far away these days. This is My gift to you. You have My peace and joy. You are called to let Me work in your soul just as I work in your daily routine.

My child, I always ask you to *leave everything to God* through Me, that way much more is being accomplished and you are at peace.

I let you into My Heart. May I be at home in your heart? Pray! I bless you. Peace."

"My child, fear nothing."

Oct. 10–"My child, I shall always respond to My children when they call on Me. I am full of tender mercy for sinners.

My child, in spite of all your frailties I am still holding out to you My Immaculate Heart. It only waits for your response of faith and trust and it is My good pleasure to give you My grace and blessing.

My child, fear nothing. I shall always come to your aid when you call. I bless you. Pray!"

"Help everyone."

Oct. 12–"My dear child, I am letting you come very close to Me. You are granted special grace in this.

My child, I accept all that you give Me and love that which comes from your heart.

My child, please continue to pray. With your prayer you *help everyone* and I am happy. I bless you. Peace."

"With Me you have everything you need."

Oct. 13–"My dear child. Am I not always the one that holds you up even though you think the matter is beyond Me? But you don't know then your Mother as well as you should.

This is why half the time you are uneasy about everything and the other half trying to sort it all out by yourself, and not even once turning to Heaven for help - as if only everything depended on you!

Therefore I tell you, *with Me you have everything you need*. Pray. Don't worry. Pray. Don't be looking for impossible answers. Just pray and pray some more, and all your problems will go away. Pray. I bless you."

"I wish to draw souls."

Oct. 14–"My dear child! How fortunate you are to be blessed by God with such things as My close contact with you.

I wish to draw souls through this contact to a deeper awareness of My love for all My children. Pray! Pray! Pray!"

"Be truthful with yourself."

Oct. 15–"Hello My child. You are very slow to grasp that Satan is only waiting to make you fall, thus he is ready to throw all kinds of accusations at you and therefore you are left so much feeling discouraged.

Don't you know My power is such that, if you allow Me, I can shoo him away and let you rest in My arms with joy. You have your own will to *be truthful with yourself.*

I am letting you see how much power you have when you give your heart to Me. My joy is to see you chase Satan away with your prayer. Pray. Pray. Pray."

"Always be happy to pray!"

Oct. 22–"My child, God will always bless you because you wish only to do His will.

It is better to lift your heart to Me than to open it to worldly comfort.

My child always be at peace, thus you know where your true joy comes from and have complete trust in how and where I lead you. *Always be happy to pray!"*

"Recreate an atmosphere of faith."

Oct. 23–"Hello My little one! Am I so loving that you are so happy to hear Me in your heart? This gift is My special blessing. Thank God for this. I am helping you along the road to holiness.

Don't you know I am letting you recognise the little petals that fall to My feet? Don't you want to pick them up? Thus you are made aware of My special care of you. My child, I draw you into solitude to let you look into My Heart.

But what I give you, you are to ponder in your heart, thus you *recreate an atmosphere of faith* in your soul.

Pray and do all with Me, even though you find sometimes you have nothing to do. Then do what you can to help others, thus you fill up treasure in Heaven and I take it to My Heart and keep it forever safe for you. Pray! I bless you."

"Do not worry about anything."

Oct. 25–"My child, I am with you in whatever you do. I am holding you and giving you strength.

I would be very happy if you would abandon yourself more so as you *do not worry about anything.* Therefore you may run the way to God in complete trust and evangelical simplicity and joy.

My child, to be so full of My Heavenly sweetness brings only your true joy. Pray! Pray! Pray!"

"God knows all your difficulties."

Oct. 26–"My child, *God knows all your difficulties*. You are asked to carry them with love – to be little – thus Satan has no chance to draw near, and I lead you in true peace, and you receive My grace. Pray! Always!"

"Do your best."

Oct. 27–"Hello My little one, don't be afraid of failure. It is in trying that God blesses you.

Do your best. Run the race to the end and do your best to be good. My child, I will do the rest.

Now cry no more with discouragement. It is only Satan trying to make everything seem wrong and thus fill you with helplessness.

Think of Me and how I am seeing to it that you are given My hand and special love. Pray! Pray! Pray! I bless you."

"Make a firm commitment."

Oct. 28–"Dear child, so few realise how much danger their souls are in. Thus Satan assures them longevity of life thus preventing them in seeing the urgent need of their souls. I am crying for such souls to return to the path of grace.

If you are a little unsure and you think you may be of such a state that you worry about your soul, *make a firm commitment* to go to Mass and receive – Properly!

My child, your life here on earth is short. I want you to only do as I wish, that is, pray.

If you are slow to understand what I am doing, accept your lack of understanding, and give it up to God through Me. Continue to pray."

"Bless yourself with Holy Water more."

Oct. 28–"My child, I hold out My Heart. Never think there is no place for you in it.

Bless yourself with Holy Water more. My child, I love you. I bless you. Peace."

"Be at peace about everything."

Oct. 29–"My child, I do not want you to ingratiate yourself with this world, but seek the way of humility under My Mantle.

My child, I also don't want you worrying about your temporal life, but *be at peace about everything* and God, who sees your heart, will reward you."

"I open to you My Heart."

Oct. 29–"Dear child, *I open to you My Heart*. I want you to know that Satan is very powerful. My child, call Me often.

You so seldom do these days. Thus Satan fills your heart with perversities, but I watch over you, My little one.

Thus I remind you to invoke Me and ask for My most powerful intercession, thus your heart is safe under My Mantle. I bless you. Pray!"

"In My hands, everything turns to gold."

Oct. 30–"Dear child. Wine that has failed is worth nothing, so too are simple acts done purely for applause. That is why I want you to pray that you do everything for Me.

My child, *in My hands, everything turns to gold* and is sublime to God. Therefore I ask that when you begin anything, look at Me to help. Pray! I bless you."

"Don't be annoyed at anything."

Oct. 30–"Dear child, I tell you, don't worry – just pray and be at peace. I know you find it all so hard at times, but I am still loving you.

Don't be annoyed at anything. Let Me settle everything as you've seen today. Pray. I bless you."

"I want always prayer in your heart."

Oct. 31–"My dear child, I want you to be always ready to give Me your heart even when you find your cross heavy. It is when you do this you become very beautiful. This is a secret.

I want always prayer in your heart and joy in all the trials of your life.

I ask that you trust in Me no matter how agitated your heart becomes. Thus you help yourself to be at peace and I am thus unhindered in coming to you. Pray! I bless you."

"Always be little."

Nov. 2–"Dear child, I am giving you a new awareness of joy under My Maternal love. It is to help you live with faith and love and kindness towards all. Thus you help Me with so much, and I am able to move more easily through your day.

My child, *always be little,* wanting only the gift – this message – nothing else. I will give you a special blessing on the *8th of December*. I bless you. Pray!"

"I don't want you full of fear."

Nov. 3–"Dear child, I want you to tell Me all that you may wish and be happy. You will always find in Me a recess of peace.

My child, you should seek only the way that I lead you. *I don't want you full of fear,* thus your heart becomes sad and your Rosary loses much. You should pray with joy.

I am full of charm and I fill your empty heart with My love when I come and give you affection. I am peaceful and always smiling at you.

I know the night of your suffering seems long, but I lighten it for you. Be like a child in My arms, thus you remain little and see Me with the eyes of faith. I am sorry for arriving late. I bless you. Pray!"

"I hold your future."

Nov. 4–"My dear child, rest in My Immaculate Heart whenever the darkness of this world becomes too great for you. I am therefore able to hide you under My Holy Mantle and you think only of how I am loving you. This will give your soul new life and light, thus you see things as they really are.

My child, be always letting Me plan your every moment, thus I give you a peace about everything and you're less inclined to be fearful of everything.

Remember, *I hold your future* in My hand. You must actively abandon your life to Me! Pray. I bless you."

"To be sure of Heaven take My hand."

Nov. 6–"My dear child. I want you to remember always that it is God's love that gives you true joy.

They that put all they have into earthly vessels are being so foolish as to think it will last forever. If they would realise I am the only true treasury that holds safe everything that is left in Me. Therefore, when you want *to be sure of Heaven, take My hand.*

My child, I settle all your little troubles, thus you are able to continue in peace with devotion to Me. I bless you. Pray!"

"Be at peace about everything."

Nov. 7–"My dear little one, why do you still become impatient with Me? Don't I move only because God allows it?

You are invited to *be at peace about everything*. Thus you do what I want, and I don't have to keep reminding you of how things should be.

My child, I look at you and My hand guides you slowly along the path to Heaven. I can't be always inviting you to be abandoned if you are not opening to Me your heart and accepting all God sends you with love. Pray! I thank you for coming."

"Unnecessary worrying is useless."

Nov. 10–"Dear child, I don't want you thinking of things that are of a petty nature.

Think of only My peace and how I let you see that in Me is all peace. You should be on guard to see to it that I hold you safe and nothing else will give you the light that I give you. This is why you are at times so undisturbed.

My child, all *unnecessary worrying is useless* and leads you to despair, thus you lose the joy of My countenance.

My child, it is in prayer that you will gain all. This is why I call you. So please continue, no matter if you find your soul becomes dark for no reason. Continue to pray. I bless you."

"I am always close."

Nov. 10–"My child, look at Me whenever you feel lost, and I will give you My deep calm, and you will in your heart know *I am always close.*

Pray. Pray. Pray. I am with you always and I smile at you. Have faith. Don't let go of Me."

"Treat yourself with kindness."

Nov. 11–"My little one, I am always with love, hour after hour, close by.

You should *treat yourself with kindness* and cease to think I have nothing to tell you when you are sick.

Priests are continually plagued by Satan if you don't offer to Me your suffering. Pray. I bless you."

"Thank God in His mercy."

Nov. 12–"Dear child, greet the morning – indeed every morning – with a smile. That way you lift your soul and I am happy.

Child! why do you wish for all your trials to go? Are they not your way to Heaven and don't they give you a dignity beyond your worth – that Jesus allows you to carry the Cross with Him?

My child, suffering is also a time of reflection where you are tied down and you are allowed to think. Take full advantage of this.

What you have is a time to stop rushing around and to take a look at all, including your own soul. *Thank God in His mercy.* Pray. I bless you."

"Now is the time for prayer."

Nov. 14–"My dear child. Why do you constantly give your heart up to despondency? Am I not doing everything? Is it not Me who gives you peace? Then why do you trouble yourself so much when I am asking you to let Me lead you even though you cannot see your way ahead?

Patience My child! This is what is so much lacking in your soul. When, is to be left to God. *Now is the time for prayer.* Pray! I bless you."

"Pray My Rosary."

Nov. 15–"Dear child, I am protecting you these days. Accompany Me and thank Me for the graces I give you. My child, you may tell the Priest the secrets!

I want you to continue in praying My Rosary. I recommend it especially and it will win many graces for you, thus My embrace.

My child prayer, Oh! prayer is so pleasing to God. His mercy is opened anew especially when you pray My Rosary. *Pray My Rosary*. I bless you."

"God wants your heart."

Nov. 16–*'Why do You come?'*
"Dear child, I come to guide you and tell you that *God wants your heart*. Offer it through Me.

Dear child, I am letting you taste the sweet and delicate life in your soul. But, if you are to really receive that which God wishes to intimate, you must put away all grossness and life must be lived after the spirit. Pray. I bless you."

"Tell the Priest."

Nov. 19–"Dear child, *tell the Priest* to get the Medal* struck as I have shown you."

* See page 621

"Only God is truth."

Nov. 25–"Dear child, pray with love My Rosary, thus you draw down God's Mercy and I am very happy.

Dear child, be slow to draw credence to all that the world makes to be true. *Only God is truth.**

Dear child, I want you to have in your heart whenever you doubt and are afraid, that I hold you, thus nothing will harm you. Pray! Pray! Pray!"

---

* Psalm 139 All knowing

"Don't worry."

Nov. 26–"Dear child, I, your Mother, am making everything ready. *Don't worry* about the slowness of your Confessor, I am helping him.

Dear child, it is time you put away all that would make you fearful about what I am asking of you. I am helping you in this.

Pray. Continue in love. I bless you."

"Pray much."

Nov. 27–"Dear child, thank you for doing as I asked. I don't want you lacking in faith in what I tell you. This is My joy to see you in wonder at what I am doing here. Thus you grow in confidence in My Immaculate Heart.

Dear child, I invite you to *pray much* so as you help My Son and you cause many to come back – even those most distant souls. Pray! I am helping you."

"Don't let anything trouble you."

Nov. 29–"Dear child, I am holding you more these days. It is My grace that you perceive in your soul, thus you are readily open to all I am giving you.

Dear child, *don't let anything trouble you*. Place no importance on little trials.

Dear child, if you are ready to respond to Me then you are moving toward Heaven. Therefore you are able to some extent see My hand in all I am doing here.

Dear child, this is how I would have you, thinking only on how I lead you. Constantly turn your heart to Me, thus you become strong in faith. Pray! Pray! Pray!"

"Leave every little thing in My hands."

Nov. 30–"Dear child, bring Me all that would disturb your soul, then you see how loving a Mother I am to you. Dear child, I know you don't think this all possible. You let so many misgivings tumble you around.

I want you to let Me act. *Leave every little thing in My hands.* It would not be possible for you to understand everything I am doing.

I ask that you pray with love and know I will never abandon you. Dear child, tell (----) I am looking at her and smiling. Pray! Pray! Pray!"

*"They that read My message
also will receive, through My Heart,
spiritual favours."*

Dec. 1–"Dear child, I wish those that read *My Message of Mercy* make known its contents, thus God may favour many more.

Dear child, write even though you do not feel worthy. Dear child, *they that read My message also will receive, through My Heart, spiritual favours,* increasing even during their temporal lives and in the glory of Heaven.

Dear child, your whole life will be a prayer to Me and you burn with love. Pray. I bless you."

"Seek only everyday My Heart."

Dec. 2–"Dear child the grace I give you will open to you a pathway to My Heart. I ask that you, whom I give My message, *seek only everyday My Heart.**

I know the miserable state which you labour under. But I invite you to simply recite this daily so that you be spiritually united with My Sorrowful and Immaculate Heart

'O Sweetest of Mothers, bless and protect us as we look to you for help.'**

Dear child, you are called by your sweet Mother. Come to Me without fear. I will help you in all that afflicts you and give you peace to move with love under My hand. Pray. I bless you."

---

* This Diary
** Recite between each decade of the Rosary.

"I am always with you."

Dec. 4–"Dear child, I tell you to pray about everything and therefore I am able to help. If you allow your trials to come to you without any aversion to them, they become a way of helping sinners convert.

Don't be always thinking I let you pass your day alone. Not a moment goes by I don't know about, so you see *I am always with you.*

Dear child, let Me step into every moment with you. Simply think I am guiding your day. Pray! Pray! Pray!"

"I come to teach you the value of prayer."

Dec. 5–"Dear child, I am your sweet Mother. I want you to lift your eyes to Me thus I am letting you come to want Heaven.

I am always thinking of My poor children who have no one to pray from their hearts for them. If only they knew how much souls need prayer.

Dear child, this is why *I come, to teach you the value of prayer,* thus you make amends for so much and great graces are given by God. Pray! Pray! Pray!"

*"I am inviting you to receive, with love,
My little petals."*

Dec. 6–"Dear child, beware! Satan is very powerful these days! To know My Heart awaits your little glances are enough to chase him away.

Dear child, *I am inviting you to receive, with love My little petals* which I send you everyday, in order that you see Me more, and earnestly seek all I am furnishing you with.

Dear child, I want you to delight My eyes when I look into your heart. I don't want to find only sadness there. Pray! Pray! Pray!"

"I am the Immaculate Conception."

Dec. 8–"Dear child –
 'I am the Immaculate Conception.'

"Be at peace."

Dec. 9–"Dear child, I don't want you worrying about thinking *'Will I suffer because of this or that.'* I know what to do. Leave everything in My hands and *be at peace*.

Dear child, don't you hear My voice? Is this not so wonderful? Let it sink deep into your heart.

Dear child, I do love you and I do know how weak you are. Nevertheless, I still love you. Pray! I bless you!"

"Listen carefully to what I have to tell you."

Dec. 11–"Dear child, *listen carefully to what I have to tell you.*

I want My Image* to be placed in honour in this Chapel; and where fixed in the City or Town whatever Church** the faith of that place will never be overthrown.

Dear child, I am calling you to simply pray. Be ready to do what I tell you and don't let this passing world hold your attention. Pray. I bless you!"

* The Image of Peace
** Parish

"Let My Maternal love guide you."

Dec. 12–"Dear child, I invite you to *let My Maternal love guide you.*"

"Pray. Pray. Pray."

Dec. 12–"Dear child, it is in letting Me act that all is accomplished. Only this is what matters that God's Will prevail in all. *Pray. Pray. Pray.*"

"Leave it to Me."

Dec. 13–"Dear child, I want to tell you not to get upset at the least scruple. *Leave it to Me.* Bright is the way I would want you to be, thus you glow with My light.

Dear child, I do know how everything is and I do know how to move. Let Me. Then you are at peace and I am very happy.

Dear child, I want you to pray with patience and don't let distraction cause you to fade. I am with you when you pray. Pray! I bless you."

"I come from Heaven."

Dec. 14–"Dear child, I wish you to light this candle in honour of My presence among you every time you meet to pray!

This is now the time when I am asking God to pour down special blessings on the world. Don't let disapproval or any kind of disappointments disturb you.

From this Chapel I am blessing you and giving you all the graces you need. Dear child, this is a holy time, a time of hope for all who look to Me.

Dear child, *I come from Heaven* to give you everything that is good. I am your Merciful Mother who looks with love on you and who pleads for you, so don't worry. Pray! I bless you."

"Remain close to Me."

Dec. 15–"Dear child, if you *remain close to Me* you will not be defeated.

Do only My loving Son's Will. Want only to please Me and you please My Son. Then God will listen to you and give you His blessing.

Dear child, you have now been allotted so much. I don't want you letting it slip from your heart! Dear child, it is I, your Mother, who holds you, thus I give you strength to continue to write. Pray. I bless you."

"I plead for you."

Dec. 16–"Dear child, I look on you with love. Don't ever think I dislike you because you are weak. No! *I plead for you* all the more to the throne of God. Actually, I ask God to give you grace. I am your Mother and through Me comes all grace.

Dear child, Hell is enraged at what I do for you. Dear child, love simply, then you see My beauty and Satan cannot harm you.

Dear child, do not think I draw you just to protect you, I draw you because you are most in need. Pray! I bless you."

"Help Me save them."

Dec. 17–"Dear child, have I not told you I am present when you meet to pray?

Dear child, to know My peace is a gift. Let your heart want this and you will want Heaven.

Dear child, I love poor sinners. *Help Me save them* by your devotion to Me. Pray! I bless you."

"This is why I come."

Dec. 18–"Dear child, I am so sad. Many proclaim from their lips devotion to Me but in their hearts only the world holds their attention. Poor sinners, such ridicule! I cry so much for them. Pray for them.

You are called to pray with Me. I want you to open your heart to Me so that you feel somewhat My loving impatience to reconcile them with My Son. Dear child, the day of joy is saddened for Me because of them.

Dear child, *this is why I come,* that through Me God may look with pardon on those that most offend Him during this holy time.* Pray! I will give a special smile just for you on the day of love."

---

* Advent

"Let Me act."

Dec. 20–"Dear child, let My hand guide you through each day, that way I am ready to pour light into your darkest hours.

Dear child, don't be sad when I ask you to open up to Me. God wants you to respond to what I wish to do here but only if you *let Me act*.

Dear child, you are a building which I am making strong. Only when you leave everything in My hands will the building be held up. Pray! Pray! Pray!"

"So many waste hours."

Dec. 23–"Dear child, why do you think I call you over to *My Chapel*? It is because I really come.

Dear child, don't entertain anything that is of too worldly a nature for too long. *So many waste hours* in this way and only bring sorrow to My Heart.

Dear child, I wait with open arms for you always. Pray! I bless you."

"I settle everything."

Dec. 24–"Dear child I should not have come today, but I have promised, so I do.

Dear child, you allow Satan get the better of you and allow your hurting cause you to be annoyed at yourself. This is not to be the way I want you. You must at these moments let Me act.

Dear child I need to tell you again, *I settle everything* for you if you let Me. Pray! I bless you."

"I am very happy to see you at My feet."

Dec. 25–"Dear child. God wishes you a peaceful and holy blessing upon you and your home at this time.

Dear child, *I am very happy to see you at My feet.* I bless you. May God's Peace reign in your home, now and always.

Dear child, pray much for all your needs to *Our Lady Queen of the Home* thus Her loving eyes give you peace of heart.

Dear child, I have shown you where I wish the new Image. I wish this new Image should bring peace to every Home, every Convent, every Church, Hospital, School. In fact I wish it bring peace wherever it is placed. Pray. I bless you."

"Let nothing cause you to be afraid."

Dec. 26–"Dear little one, I invite you always *let nothing cause you to be afraid.*

I take you in My arms, thus you are made aware of My peace. Dear child, it is in letting Me into your heart that everything is calmed for you.

Dear child, I always wait for your invitation. It is only when you want Me that I can help you. Pray! Pray! Pray!"

"Respond to My grace."

Dec. 27–"Dear child, why do you doubt My kindness towards you? Do you not yet perceive that I am from Heaven, and so free from how men weigh everything, dividing everything up into anomalies, thus never looking into the hearts of men!

Dear child, I want you to *respond to My grace*. It will lead you to a true value of things, letting you see that only the haughty fall and the humble are exalted in the end.

Dear child, this is why I come, to teach you how to look at what I do, thus you come close to Heaven. Pray. I bless you."

"I stand between Earth and Heaven."

Dec. 28–"Hello My dear child. Do you still think that I would abandon you?

Let My new Image give you hope. Invoke Me often. Dear child, My new Image will stand as a reminder of My closeness to My Son as I look to earth hoping that My children would look to Me. Thus I dispense God's grace on all who ask for My help.

Dear child, *I stand between Earth and Heaven* pleading on behalf of poor men, seeking to help them in all their needs thus gaining for them the graces necessary for their salvation. Pray! Pray! Pray!"

"I am really here."

Dec. 29–"Dear child, I wish to have you in no doubt as to My loving presence with you! *I am really here!* Dear child, how I leave you with My peace should be a clear sign to you of My gift.

Dear child, I don't want you letting little earthly troubles make you lose faith in what I am giving you here. Everything is in God's plan.

Don't you know that I act when you least expect it, thus I counter-balance all of your doubts and once more restore your faith that I am here with you! Pray! Pray! Pray!"

"I come that I may smile on you."

Dec. 30–"Dear child, I invite you to seek My Heart for all your comfort.

Dear child, My Heart is a place of peace for all My children who are saddened by the oppression of this world.

Dear child, this is why *I come, that I may smile on you,* thus you are left with God's peace in your heart. Pray! Pray! Pray!"

My name is----
'The Merciful Madonna.'

Jan. 1–"My little one, *My name is*----
'The Merciful Madonna.'

The Way of Meekness

For little souls the way of spiritual impoverishment

Utilise God's great compassion through Our Lady's Heart. You have nothing of yourself, but expect everything because you have Mary. Make this *Act of Perfect Surrender* every morning and evening for the sake of poor sinners.

My Angel.

An Act of Perfect Surrender to God through the Merciful Madonna

Merciful Madonna, I consecrate myself to Thee. Help me. I give Thee charge of my soul both now and in Eternity. Clothe me with Your Holy Mantle. Have mercy on me and grant me the gift I now ask for (*to be one of Your little souls.*) I beg Thee comfort me at the hour of my death and may I die in peace. Amen.

O Virgin defend me all pure and sweet.   3 times

"My little one, there is no place in the whole world where you will find true happiness, only with Me in Heaven."

June 12 1989

The Scapular of Mary Immaculate Mediatrix of all graces

This scapular was revealed by Our Lady on March 25 1992, the year of the Fatima 75th Jubilee.

"My little one! to all who wear this scapular faithfully, I promise to grant, before they die, the last Sacraments of the Church. This shall be the sign of your consecration to My Immaculate Heart!"

Sept. 5 1992

This one-piece scapular is made with blue cord and royal blue felt, bordered with gold thread.

Novena to
Our Lady Queen of the Home *
From 14$^{th.}$ - 22nd August.

For recitation on ordinary rosary beads

Begin with:
The Creed----------------One Our Father
One Hail Mary-----------One Glory Be

On the large beads: 3 times
O Virgin defend me all pure and sweet.

On the small beads:
Our Lady Queen of the Home, Pray for us.

Conclude with:
Hail Holy Queen

* See messages August 22 and 23

"Dear children, I do love you infinitely. Don't be sad if your life is not filled with Divine favours. It is not this that is important. What is important is that you persevere in prayer and do not give in when life becomes hurtful. I am the Blessed Mother who shall come in the midst of all your misfortunes and keep you safe. You should know this. Be as good as you can. Live in faith all I tell you. Pray. Pray. Pray
April 26 1992

"Pray! Where the Image is exposed and venerated My Immaculate Heart will bestow many graces of conversion. Do not let a day go by without at least turning once to the Image praying-

Mary Immaculate,
I beg of You, obtain pardon for me
and I ask, through Your Immaculate Heart,
save us from sin and lead all to Heaven.

As many times as you say this you will be saving a sinner."
January 21 1995

For Priests

The Blessed Mother would like Priests to keep these messages in their hearts and if they accept the requests they will receive the promises.

My Angel

1. *"You will always find in Me a recess of peace."*

2. *"I look upon you as My very own."*

3. *"Surrender yourself to Me, thus you will be made strong by My love."*

4. *"Place all your merits in My hands and let everything that happens be a way of offering up in obedience to Me."*

5. *"The time will come when you will no longer need to rationalise what is happening."*

6. *"By My hand guarding you, I hold back so much that would harm you."*

7. *"I want My Image to be placed in honour in this Chapel* and where fixed in City or Town, whatever Church** the faith of that place will never be overthrown."*

*Oratory of the Immaculate Heart, Raheny, Dublin.

** The promise only applies when it is placed solemnly in the Church of that locality.

My Angel

The Promises for Priests

1. People will see God in them.

2. They themselves will receive great blessings from God.

3. They will receive the zeal to be totally abandoned to God and be of one mind with Him.

My Angel

Special Message

"The Book of Messages I have given you is essentially the Message I wish to give to every soul, that is, including the souls of Priests. In essence the Book of Messages is for the renewal of every soul. Providence will reveal to every soul how best they should be spread. That is, in the manner in which they feel it in their soul how it should be spread, as this is shown to each soul. Only thus will each soul receive the blessing of the Message if they spread it. If not no blessing will be received."

April 2 1998

"The more the Church looks at Mary the more She will honour Me."
Our Lord 1997

The Medal

See page 621

On the fear of Hell

Our Lady said:-

"My child, it is like this, if you wish to fear Hell, all you have to do is think of the desolation of that place and that it is the final abode of that soul that chooses such a place."

Sept. 1993

Consecration to solemnly bless a Parish before the Image of Peace

Holy Virgin, we consecrate our Parish to You through Your Image of Peace. We wish to establish in our Parish a tender devotion to You, *The Merciful Madonna,* and as Your children, we offer to You all our joys and sufferings. We beg Your Motherly blessing on our Parish and the promise You made when You said ----- *"I want My Image to be placed in honour in this Chapel and where fixed in City or Town-- whatever Church--* the faith of that place will never be overthrown."* This we ask this through Christ our Lord. Amen

*The promise only applies when it is placed solemnly in the Church of that locality.

Introduction to the Cantons

Our Lady wishes to have communities of prayer or cantons where the messages of *Our Lady's Message of Mercy to the World* are read during the Rosary so that the messages come alive.

E.g. Canton of a road or section of a community.

Revealed by Our Lady May 14 1992

Purpose of a Canton

"Dear little one, I wish to gather around My Immaculate Heart a vast amount of valiant little souls.* I will truly form them Myself hidden enclosed under My Holy Mantle.** My little one I wish to draw them from the ranks of the lowest and even from the ranks of My predilected. I wish them to hide under My Mantle in humility, consecrated to Me in a special way.*** I will Myself consecrate them in the spiritual way. Thank you for coming." December 8 1991

* Prayer groups: ** The Scapular of Mary Immaculate
*** Consecration according to St. Louis de Montfort

"Dear Children! your vitality must come from your devotion to Me, thus you become more and more like My Son. Live My messages then you cause that change of heart where before no change was possible. Do not, dear children, move away from My Motherly invitation but move towards your Mother who looks to your every need. Your vocation today is to be My Apostles through your wonder of all that I am doing among you. My Motherly Heart, dear children, calls you to this dynamic apostolate* so much needed today. I bless you. Pray." Dec. 7 1992

* To pray the Rosary and spread the Messages.

Reason for the Canton

"I want that you pray everyday and to thank God for the graces He is giving you through My coming to you. Thank Divine Providence, for without it you would not be here. Yes my child, I know the world is crude, but it is through your devotion to My Immaculate Heart can you put things right with God. God Himself desires this devotion that it should save many sinners and find its greatest fulfilment in the means I am giving you here, as at Fatima. Not only did I call then, but I call again today, here, that the reality of the Gospel message be once again made known. Do not worry. Pray, and hold on to your belief in God. God must come first that He may fill your emptiness with which the world cannot fill. God can do this if you pray. If not, your faith will become indifferent but God will still be there, this is the reality I am giving you. Holiness is for all of you, but it is up to you to use the resources God gives you, that is prayer and reparation. Give God His due honour and He will bless you, this is why you were given life. Thank you for coming."

Sept. 8 1996

How to set up a Canton or Prayer group

A Priest or a layperson may set up a canton. It can be set up anywhere preferably with the approval of the Parish Priest. Its aim and first and last rule—*Pray the Rosary*.

The Canton of Our Lady Queen of the Home
is the name for each prayer group.

Altar for the Canton

"You are to put only the new Image*
on the altar when you meet to pray My canton,
including candle, flowers and crucifix.
Thank you."

September 19 2004

* The Image of Peace

CANTON OF
Our Lady Queen of the Home

"Make no additions to this canton."

Our Lady September 22 2004

This is the format approved by Our Lady.

Our Lady's promise

*"Dear child, I am present at every canton
no matter where it is in the world.
It is through your devotion at each canton
you help Me save poor sinners."*

August 21 2004

Prayers of the Canton

In the name of the Father, and of the Son, and of the Holy Spirit. Amen.

Immaculate Heart of Mary, Mother of God, Queen of Heaven and Earth, we humbly beseech You from the bottom of our hearts to be with us this evening. Please invite Jesus, Your precious Son, sweet Mother, so that we may find shelter in His Sacred Heart. Help us with these cantons so that we may offer to You God the Father, Son and Holy Spirit, with all the choirs of Angels and all the Saints, the tribute of our devotion and love. Amen.

An Act of Perfect Surrender to God through the Merciful Madonna

(You are invited to kneel before the altar of the Merciful Madonna)

Merciful Madonna I consecrate myself to Thee. Help me. I give Thee charge of my soul both now and in Eternity. Clothe me with Your Holy Mantle. Have mercy on me and grant me the gift I now ask for (to be one of Your little souls.) I beg Thee comfort me at the hour of my death and may I die in peace. Amen.

O Virgin defend me all pure and sweet.   3 times

Prayer to the Holy Spirit

Come Holy Spirit fill the hearts of the faithful and enkindle in them the fire of Thy love. Send forth Thy spirit and they shall be created and Thou shall renew the face of the earth. O God, who by the light of the Holy Spirit, did instruct the hearts of the faithful, grant that by the power of the Holy Spirit, we may be truly wise and courageous in following the Gospel, and use our charismatic gifts to the full in preparing the way for the coming of Thy Kingdom. We make this prayer through Christ Our Lord. Amen.

Hymn to Our Lady Mary Immaculate Mediatrix of all Graces

(Official air by the late Stella Maris Lilley)
May also be sung to the air—Hail Glorious St. Patrick.

O Virgin defend me, all pure and sweet.
O Mary my Mother, I kneel at Your feet.
To guide us to Heaven, You teach us to pray,
Immaculate Mother be with me today.

O Virgin defend me, all pure and sweet.
O Mary my Mother, I kneel at Your feet.
I hide 'neath Your Mantle, all care set apart,
O Mother of Mercy, I give You my heart.

Chaplet of Divine Love

For the Pope and the conversion of Russia

Our Father---Hail Mary---Glory be—

On the beads before each decade:

Saviour of the world through Your Divine Love save us and save the whole world.

On the ten Hail Mary beads:

V/ O my Jesus.
R/ I trust in Your Divine Love.

Finish with:

I believe, I hope, and I trust in Your Divine Love. Save us and save the whole world.   3 times

---

For peace in our hearts---- Our Father-
For peace in the world----- Glory be-

St. Michael Prayer

St. Michael, the Archangel, defend us in the hour of battle. Be our safeguard against the wickedness and snares of the Devil. May God restrain him, we humbly pray, and do thou, O Prince of the Heavenly Host, by the power of God, thrust Satan down to Hell, and with him all the evil spirits who wander through the world for the ruin of souls. Amen.

Now pause for a moment in silence to leave everything to God.

Recitation of the Holy Rosary

For the Triumph of the Immaculate Heart
and the conversion of poor sinners

Begin with the Creed

Before each decade read a message from the diary
"Our Lady's Message of Mercy to the World"

After each Glory be—

O My Jesus, forgive us our sins. Save us from the fires of Hell. Lead all souls to Heaven, especially those most in need of Thy Mercy.

"O Sweetest of Mothers, bless and protect us as we look to You for help"

December 2 1989

Optional:

O Virgin defend me all pure and sweet.

V/ Mary Immaculate, I beg of You, obtain pardon for me and I ask through Your Immaculate Heart

R/ save us from sin and lead all to Heaven.

Dearest Mother, with these golden chains we bind our families to Your Immaculate Heart.

After the *Hail Holy Queen,* someone stands and holds a Crucifix aloft and a prayer is recited for

The Triumph of the Holy Cross

God all powerful, who has suffered on the tree of the Cross, be with us.

Holy Cross of Jesus Christ, have pity on us.

Holy Cross of Jesus Christ, be our hope.

Holy Cross of Jesus Christ, turn away from us all sharp weapons.

Holy Cross of Jesus Christ, pour into us all good.

Holy Cross of Jesus Christ, turn away from us all evil.

Holy Cross of Jesus Christ, make us well in the paths of salvation.

Holy Cross of Jesus Christ, preserve us from all spiritual and temporal accidents.

Holy Cross of Jesus Christ, may I adore Thee.

Holy Cross of Jesus Christ, now and forever.

Jesus of Nazareth, crucified, have pity on us. Make the invisible fly far from us, now and for ever and ever. Amen.

(Holy Mary, Mother of God, St. Joseph, St. Michael the Archangel and the Holy Angels protect us.)

Now the Crucifix is kissed

Novena for Our Lady's intentions

To die to ourselves. To understand why Our Lady does not deal with us as we think in human terms and for all who do not seek Jesus crucified.

Nine *Hail Marys* followed by

May the Sacred Heart of Jesus be praised, glorified and loved today and everyday throughout the whole world, now and forever. Amen

---

For peace in our Households

(You are invited to kneel as an act of reparation.)

On the beads before each decade:

Lord, teach the whole world how to suffer in union with You.

On the ten *Hail Mary* beads:

V/ Mary Immaculate, I beg of You, obtain pardon for me and I ask through Your Immaculate Heart

R/ save us from sin and lead all to Heaven.

Prayer for the Legion of Mary

Our Father---three Hail Marys

Our Lady, Mediatrix of all Graces, be blessed on earth as You are in Heaven. May I take delight in Your company during my day and may You chase Satan away with Your glances now and at the hour of my death. Amen

V/ You who stand between Earth and Heaven
R/ Save us. Amen.

Conclusion of Hymn

O Virgin defend me all pure and sweet.
O Mary my Mother, I kneel at Your feet.
You guide us and bless us with Your gentle touch,
O Mary I need You and love You so much.

O Virgin defend me all pure and sweet.
O Mary my Mother, I kneel at Your feet.
You know every dream, every wish You can see,
O smile on our Nation and smile upon me.

Consecration before the Image of Peace
(You are invited to kneel)

Holy Mary Mother of God, we consecrate ourselves and our families to You, through Your Image of Peace. We give You our past, present and future. We beg of You, dear Mother, the gift of peace so much needed today for ourselves and for the whole world. May Your Image of Peace do as You have said—*"I wish this new Image should bring peace to every home, every convent, every church, hospital, school in fact I wish it bring peace wherever it is placed. Pray! I bless you."* This we ask through Christ Our Lord . Amen.

The Chaplet to be prayed before the Image of Peace
Our Lady's request
Our Father---Hail Mary---Glory be--

On the beads before each decade:
Our Lady, Mediatrix of all Graces, be blessed on earth as You are in Heaven. May I take delight in Your company during my day and may You chase Satan away with Your glances now and at the hour of my death. Amen.

On the ten Hail Mary beads:
V/ You who stand between Earth and Heaven
R/ Save us. Amen

End with: O Virgin defend us all pure and sweet.
3 times

The Magnificat

My soul glorifies the Lord, My Spirit rejoices in God My Saviour. He looks on His servant in Her lowliness, henceforth all ages will call Me blessed. The Almighty works marvels for Me. Holy is His name. His mercy is from age to age on those who fear Him. He puts forth His arm in strength and scatters the proud hearted. He casts the mighty from their thrones and raises the lowly. He fills the starving with good things, sends the rich away empty. He protects Israel His servant remembering His mercy, the mercy promised to our fathers, to Abraham and his sons forever.

Glory be to the Father and to the Son and to the Holy Spirit, as it was in the beginning, is now and ever shall be, world without end Amen.

In the name of the Father and of the Son
and of the Holy Spirit. Amen.

Our Lady invites each one to receive a personal "pearl" from the diary.

One Hail Mary -is recommended prior to opening the diary.

"My child I can now tell you of My plan, the plan that began for you on the day Sept. 12 1988 which the church dedicates to My name. I came on this day or rather God chose this day to show that I am One and the same Mary who has saved the Church so many times and given it My most powerful protection. I came on this day to renew and remind the Church of My many Victories, which I will renew in your day. This day I chose in direct response to an action taken by Satan not a thousand miles from your City (Dublin)-- an action which you see before you the result and will see, because on this day a movement began to revamp the present evil propaganda to a greater autonomy in the world guided by rich and powerful men who in turn have only one aim- the destruction of the One Holy Catholic Apostolic Church! This day I chose as a proof of My constant vigilance against all error. My Child I bless you."

October 6 1993

THE FIVE MAIN COMPONENTS OF THIS DEVOTION
As revealed by my Angel today Nov.20 '06
at Our Lady's request.

1. THE IMAGE OF PEACE:

Our Lady's gift to Churches, Hospitals, Schools and Homes etc.

2. THE MIRACULOUS IMAGE:

Our Lady's personal gift to everyone that they may carry it on them as a little devotional card.

3. THE SCAPULAR:

Our Lady's mantle
To be worn around the neck for protection.
This Scapular incorporates the head and shoulders of the small miraculous Image.

4. THE DIARY:

Our Lady's "Heart"
A little blue book containing the original message.

5. THE MEDAL:

Our Lady's medallion
The centre-piece of a Rosary.

Appendix

Spirit of the Devotion

It is desired that every thing be done in a spirit of filial trust in obedience to Our Lady and that nothing be added or deleted from the new edition of the diary without the express permission of the Spiritual Director and the express permission of Our Lady.

New printing of the Book

No book / scapular / image should be sold. No new book should be printed without the express permission of the new Spiritual Director. No money is to be sent unless as approved by the Spiritual Director to any personal account.

Cost and Management

It is advisable to set up a proper committee concerning proper handling of money through the Spiritual Director. No personal account can be allowed. Committees must amount to seven or more members.

Orders of Books

Orders of books/scapulars/images must not exceed demand of volunteers on the ground in order to deliver on time.

As revealed by my Angel on June 26 2006 in Dubrovnik at Our Lady's request.

Index

A

598......Act of Reparation
156......Allow Me be your…
468......All will be well
380......All you need do…
594......An Act of Perfect…
482......Always be happy to…
506......Always be little
622......Appendix

B

176......Be always at peace
554......Be at peace
496......Be at peace about…
514......Be at peace about…
204......Be available to My…
 52......Be but patient
248......Be longing always for…
288......Be on guard not…
114......Be patient and trust…
428......Be still and wait
480......Be truthful with yourself
200......Be with Me in…
124......Become small
324......Begin anew
110......Being little entails being…
 60......Believe it is I
448......Believe this extraordinary favour
494......Bless yourself with holy…

374......Bring Me all the…
 88......Build in your soul…
246......But I love you…

C

605......Cantons- Introduction to the…
611......Cantons –Prayers of…
 22......Come closer to Me
 34......Come to Me in…
364......Come to Me in trust
 14......Come to the foot…
604......Consecration to solemnly bless…
 82......Continue to listen
270......Continue to pray
 48......Continue to pray let…

D

598......Dear children I do…
 46......Dear little one don't…
196......Decide to want to…
268......Did you notice a…
440......Discover My great gentleness
272......Do not abandon the…
328......Do not be afraid…
212......Do not become heavy…
378......Do not fear anything
 30......Do not hide from…
 94......Do not let Satan…
486......Do not worry about…
490......Do your best
502......Don't be annoyed at…
104......Don't be annoyed when…

470......Leave everything to God
562......Leave it to Me
118 ......Let it come from...
574......Let Me act
322......Let Me calm every...
422......Let Me revive it...
178 ......Let Me take all...
18 ......Let Me teach you...
424......Let My love give...
558......Let My Maternal love...
318 ......Let My messages sink...
582......Let nothing cause you...
332......Listen always to Me...
28......Listen and pray I...
556......Listen carefully to what...
214......Listen to My messages
138......Look to Me for...
406 ......Love makes up for...
1 ......Loving Me doesn't detract...

M

492......Make a firm commitment
7 ......Meaning of the Image
80......Men wish to avoid...
602......Medal The
300......Melt under My touch
252......Move within your heart
472......My child fear nothing
620......My child I can...
4........My child make reparation...
11 ......My dear little one...

42......My grace is sufficient...
282......My Immaculate Heart is...
595......My little one there...
172......My love is a...
592......My name is the Merciful Madonna
348......My plan is in...
108......My sweetness is pure...

N

74......Never tire of asking...
54......No matter how hard...
78......No one has come...
414......Nothing gives Me greater...
597......Novena to Our Lady...
524......Now is the time...

O

180......Offer even your inadequacies...
36......Offer to Me all...
16......Often you forget I...
603......On the fear of...
24......One and one only...
532......Only God is truth
130......Only God raises the...
96......Only in prayer can...
232......Only through the Rosary...
136......Open the door of...
454......Open to Me your...
436......Our Lady's Message of...
610......Our Lady's promise
388......Our Lady Queen of...

P

338......Patience My love will...
358......Pay attention to My...
390......Peace be to you
398......Place all your heartache...
86......Place your soul at...
202......Please be patient with...
346......Please hold on to...
286......Ponder in your heart...
320......Pray about all I...
302......Pray about everything
432......Pray above all for...
90......Pray and believe that...
50......Pray and long for...
128 ......Pray even if you...
292......Pray for My intentions
298......Pray for poor sinners
376......Pray for poor sinners
400 .....Pray I am smiling...
536......Pray much
526......Pray My Rosary
560......Pray Pray Pray...
228......Pray slowly take time...
372......Pray that you leave...
116......Pray trust and know...
112......Pray well
598......Pray where the Image...
426......Pray with faith
599......Priests For
600......Promises for Priests The

140......Purify your intention
606......Purpose of the Canton

R

244......Read Me again there…
607......Reason for the Canton
484......Recreate an atmosphere of…
134......Remain close to Me
566......Remain close to Me
294......Remain sweet and beautiful
 70......Renew your resolutions and…
 76......Reserve to Me the…
458......Respond I wish you…
250......Respond to Me in…
584......Respond to My grace
166......Return to the depths…

S

596......Scapular of Mary Immaculate
544......Seek only everyday My Heart
 64......Seek the way of…
404......She just smiles
122......Sinners have drifted away…
576......So many waste hours
312......Special favours will be…
600......Special Message

T

310......Take some one of…
530......Tell the Priest
522......Thank God in His Mercy
280......Thank you for the…
242......Thank you for your…

601	The more the Church...
334	The Mother of God...
542	They that read My...
144	Think of Heaven
402	This is a precious...
386	This is God's work
572	This is why I come
450	This message of Mercy...
366	Those that trust Me...
430	Thousands await this Message..
106	To be holy is...
512	To be sure of...
38	Today I have something...
438	Today I wish you...
206	To you and eventually...
520	Treat yourself with kindness

U

516	Unnecessary worrying is useless

W

594	Way of Meekness
218	What can I say...
10	What may you ask...
476	With Me you have...
40	With prayer open your...
460	With prayer you restore...

Y

462	You are My dear...
186	You are nothing without...
254	You are only too...
154	You are ready too...

258......You are safe only…
418......You are so small…
208......You are without thought…
264......You can be holy
170......You do not deceive…
224......You forget I am…
 32......You have little time…
162......You may be ridiculed…
 84......You may not understand…
132......You must allow Me…
278......You My child console Me
222......You need Me
238......You need not worry…
 98......Your only comfort is…
120......You should exercise faith
266......You should value the…

List of illustrations

  5......Our Lady visiting the Oratory…
  6......The Image of Peace
596......The Scapular of Mary Immaculate
602......The Medal